National Vital Statistics Reports

Volume 60, Number 5

May 10, 2012

Infant Mortality Statistics From the 2008 Period Linked Birth/Infant Death Data Set

by T.J. Mathews, M.S., and Marian F. MacDorman, Ph.D., Division of Vital Statistics

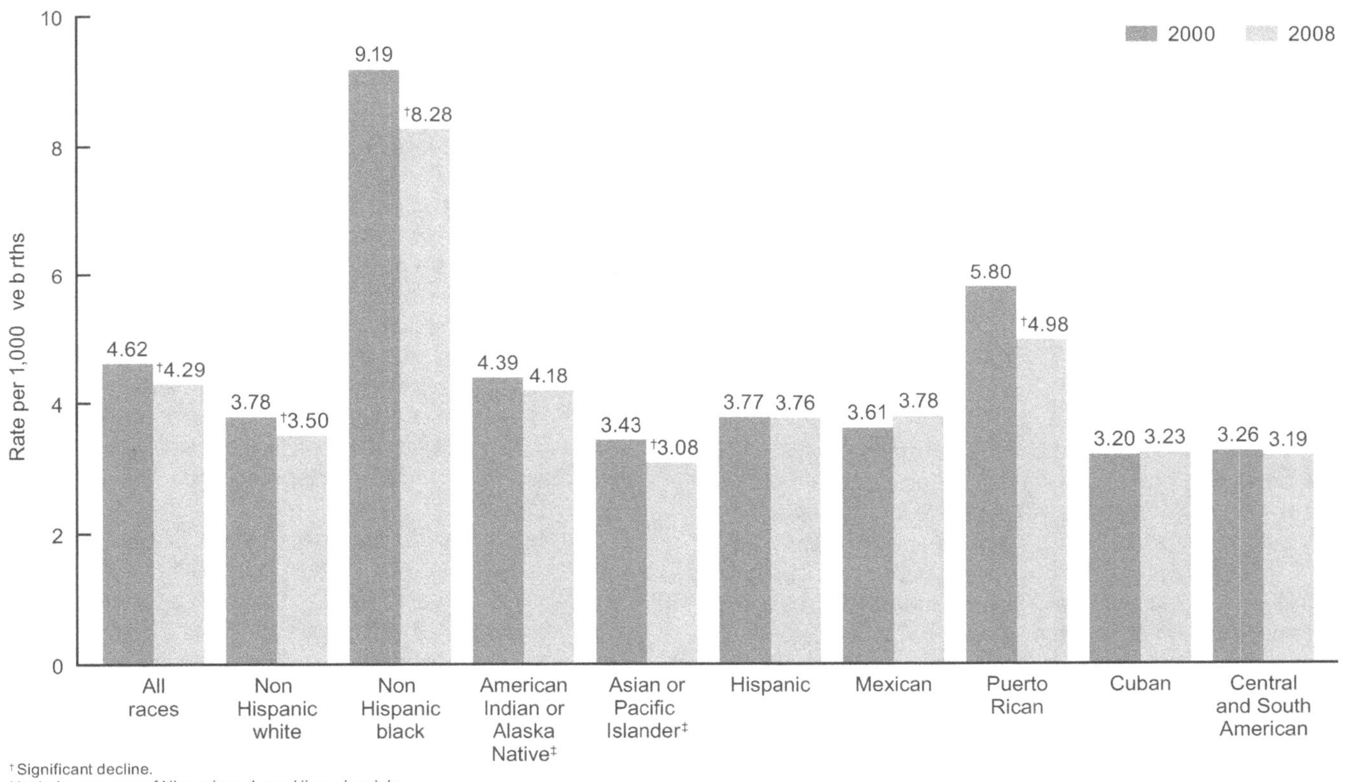

† Significant decline.
‡ Includes persons of Hispanic and non-Hispanic origin.
NOTES: Neonatal is less than 28 days. Race and Hispanic origin are reported separately on birth certificates. Race categories are consistent with the 1977 Office of Management and Budget standards. Persons of Hispanic origin may be of any race. In this figure, Hispanic women are classified only by place of origin; non-Hispanic women are classified by race. See reference 2. Thirty states reported multiple-race data on the birth certificate for 2008 and 27 for 2007. The multiple-race data for these states were bridged to the single-race categories of the 1977 standards for comparability with other states; see references 2 and 3.
SOURCE: CDC/NCHS, National Vital Statistics System.

Figure 1. Neonatal mortality rates, by race and ethnicity of mother: United States, 2000 and 2008

U.S. DEPARTMENT OF HEALTH AND HUMAN SERVICES
Centers for Disease Control and Prevention
National Center for Health Statistics
National Vital Statistics System

Abstract

Objectives—This report presents 2008 period infant mortality statistics from the linked birth/infant death data set (linked file) by a variety of maternal and infant characteristics. The linked file differs from the mortality file, which is based entirely on death certificate data.

Methods—Descriptive tabulations of data are presented and interpreted.

Results—The U.S. infant mortality rate was 6.61 infant deaths per 1,000 live births in 2008, 2 percent lower than the rate of 6.75 in 2007. Infant mortality rates ranged from 4.51 per 1,000 live births for Asian or Pacific Islander mothers to 12.67 for non-Hispanic black mothers. The rate for non-Hispanic black women declined 5 percent from 2007 to 2008. Infant mortality was higher for male infants and infants born preterm or at low birthweight. Infant mortality rates were also higher for those infants who were born in multiple deliveries, to mothers who were unmarried, and for those whose mothers were born in the 50 states or the District of Columbia. From 2007 to 2008, the neonatal mortality rate (under age 28 days) declined by 3 percent to 4.29 neonatal deaths per 1,000 live births, while the postneonatal mortality rate (aged 28 days to under 1 year) remained essentially unchanged (2.32). Preterm and low birthweight infants had the highest infant mortality rates and contributed greatly to the overall U.S. infant mortality. The three leading causes of infant death—congenital malformations, low birthweight, and sudden infant death syndrome—accounted for 46 percent of all infant deaths. In 2008, 35.4 percent of infant deaths were "preterm-related."

Keywords: infant health • birthweight • gestational age • maternal characteristics

Introduction

This report presents infant mortality data from the 2008 period linked file. In the linked file, information from the death certificate is linked to information from the birth certificate for each infant under age 1 year who died in the 50 states, District of Columbia (DC), Puerto Rico, the Virgin Islands, or Guam during 2008 (1). Linked birth/infant death data are not available for American Samoa and the Commonwealth of the Northern Marianas. The purpose of the linkage is to use the many additional variables available from the birth certificate to conduct more detailed analyses of infant mortality patterns (2,3). This report presents infant mortality data by race and Hispanic origin of the mother, birthweight, period of gestation, sex of infant, plurality, maternal age, live-birth order, mother's marital status, mother's place of birth, age at death, and underlying cause of death (Tables 1–6 and A–C, and Figures 1–5).

Data based exclusively on the vital statistics mortality file provide further information on trends in infant mortality and on causes of infant death (4). The linked file is used to analyze and calculate infant mortality rates by race and ethnicity, which are more accurately measured from the birth certificate. Some rates calculated from the mortality file differ from those published using the linked file. A more detailed discussion of these differences is presented in the "Technical Notes."

Methods

Data shown in this report are based on birth and infant death certificates registered in all states, DC, Puerto Rico, the Virgin Islands, and Guam. As part of the Vital Statistics Cooperative Program, each state provided matching birth and death certificate numbers for each infant under age 1 year who died in the state during 2008 to the Centers for Disease Control and Prevention's (CDC) National Center for Health Statistics (NCHS). When the birth and death occurred in different states, the state of death was responsible for contacting the state of birth identified on the death certificate to obtain the original birth certificate number. NCHS used the matching birth and death certificate numbers provided by the states to extract final edited data from the NCHS natality and mortality statistical files. These data were linked to form a single statistical record, thereby establishing a national linked record file.

After the initial linkage, NCHS returned lists of unlinked infant death records and records with inconsistent data between the birth and death certificates to each state. State additions and corrections were incorporated, and a final national linked file was produced. In 2008, 98.7 percent of all infant death records were successfully linked or matched to their corresponding birth records. Records were weighted to adjust for the 1.3 percent of infant death records that were not linked to their corresponding birth certificates (see "Technical Notes").

Information on births by age, race, or marital status of mother is imputed if it is not reported on the birth certificate. These items were not reported for less than 1 percent of U.S. births in 2008 (2,3).

Race and Hispanic origin are reported independently on the birth certificate. In tabulations of birth data by race and Hispanic origin, data for Hispanic persons are not further classified by race as the vast majority of women of Hispanic origin are reported as white. Data for American Indian or Alaska Native (AIAN) and Asian or Pacific Islander (API) births are not shown separately by Hispanic origin because the vast majority of these populations are non-Hispanic.

Cause-of-death statistics in this publication are classified in accordance with the *International Statistical Classification of Diseases and Related Health Problems, Tenth Revision* (ICD–10) (5) (see "Technical Notes").

This report includes data based on the 1989 and 2003 revisions of the birth certificate. Twenty-seven states and Puerto Rico implemented the 2003 revision of the U.S. Standard Certificate of Live Birth on or before January 1, 2008 (revised). These 27 states represent 65 percent of U.S. births in 2008. The remaining reporting areas include data that are based on the 1989 revision of the U.S. Standard Certificate of Live Birth (unrevised). Revised and unrevised data are combined when comparable (2,3).

Three key data items are considered noncomparable between the 1989 and 2003 revisions: trimester of pregnancy prenatal care began, maternal educational attainment, and maternal smoking during pregnancy (2,3) (see "Technical Notes"). Because infants who died in 2008 included those born in both 2007 and 2008, this report includes data on these three topics from the 22 states that implemented the 2003 revision as of January 1, 2007. Data for these limited reporting areas are shown in Table II in "Technical Notes." The 22 states include California, Colorado, Delaware, Florida, Idaho, Indiana, Iowa, Kansas, Kentucky, Nebraska, New Hampshire, New York (excluding New York city), North Dakota, Ohio, Pennsylvania, South Carolina, South

Dakota, Tennessee, Texas, Vermont, Washington, and Wyoming. Data on smoking are not available for Florida. Results for these three items from the limited reporting area are not generalizable to the country as a whole (2,3,6). These 22 states represent 53 percent of all births in 2007 (48 percent for 21 states with smoking data, which excludes Florida).

Data by maternal and infant characteristics

This report presents descriptive tabulations of infant mortality data by a variety of maternal and infant characteristics. These tabulations are useful for understanding the basic relationships between risk factors and infant mortality, *unadjusted for the possible effects of other variables.* In reality, women with one risk factor often have other risk factors as well. For example, teen mothers are more likely to be unmarried and of a low-income status, and mothers who do not receive prenatal care are more likely to be of a low-income status and uninsured. The preferred method for disentangling the multiple interrelationships among risk factors is multivariate analysis; however, an understanding of the basic relationships between risk factors and infant mortality is a necessary precursor to more sophisticated types of analyses, and is the aim of this publication.

Race and Hispanic origin data—Infant mortality rates are presented here by race and detailed Hispanic origin of mother. The linked file is particularly useful for computing accurate infant mortality rates for this purpose because the race and Hispanic origin of the mother from the birth certificate are used in both the numerator and denominator of the infant mortality rate. In contrast, for the vital statistics mortality file, race information for the denominator is the race of the mother as reported on the birth certificate, whereas the race information for the numerator is the race of the decedent as reported on the death certificate (2–4). Thus, standard infant mortality rates can be based on inconsistent information. In addition, race information from the birth certificate reported by the mother is considered to be more reliable than that from the death certificate where the race and ethnicity of the deceased infant are reported by the funeral director based on information provided by an informant or by observation.

These different reporting methods can lead to differences in race- and ethnicity-specific infant mortality rates between the two data files (4,7).

The 2003 revision of the U.S. Standard Certificate of Live Birth allows the reporting of more than one race (multiple races) for each parent (2,3,8,9). Thirty states reported multiple-race data on their birth certificates for either part or all of 2008, and 27 states in 2007. To provide uniformity and comparability of the data, multiple race is imputed to a single race; see "Technical Notes."

Statistical significance—Text statements have been tested for statistical significance, and a statement that a given infant mortality rate is higher or lower than another rate indicates that the rates are significantly different. Information on the methods used to test for statistical significance, as well as information on differences between period and cohort data, the weighting of the linked file, and a comparison of infant mortality data between the linked file and the vital statistics mortality file, are presented in "Technical Notes." Additional information on maternal age, marital status, period of gestation, birthweight, and cause-of-death classification is also presented in "Technical Notes."

Results and Discussion

Trends in infant mortality

The overall 2008 infant mortality rate from the linked file was 6.61 infant deaths per 1,000 live births, 2 percent lower than the rate of 6.75 in 2007 (Table B). The 2008 rate from the mortality file was also 6.61 (4).

The infant mortality rate declined from 1995 to 2000, plateaued from 2000 to 2005, and has declined again since then (Table B). From 2007 to 2008, the only racial or ethnic group with a significant change was non-Hispanic black women with a 5 percent decline from 13.31 to 12.67 (Table B).

Infant mortality by race and Hispanic origin of mother

In 2008 as in previous years, infant mortality rates varied considerably by race and Hispanic origin of mother (10,11). The

Table A. Infant, neonatal, and postneonatal deaths and mortality rates, by race and Hispanic origin of mother: United States, 2008 linked file

Hispanic origin and race of mother	Live births	Number of deaths			Mortality rate per 1,000 live births		
		Infant	Neonatal	Postneonatal	Infant	Neonatal	Postneonatal
Total	4,247,726	28,075	18,238	9,837	6.61	4.29	2.32
Non-Hispanic white	2,267,817	12,509	7,936	4,573	5.52	3.50	2.02
Non-Hispanic black	623,031	7,894	5,159	2,735	12.67	8.28	4.39
American Indian or Alaska Native	49,537	417	207	210	8.42	4.18	4.24
Asian or Pacific Islander	253,184	1,143	780	363	4.51	3.08	1.43
Hispanic	1,041,239	5,821	3,915	1,906	5.59	3.76	1.83
Mexican	684,883	3,822	2,588	1,234	5.58	3.78	1.80
Puerto Rican	69,015	503	344	159	7.29	4.98	2.30
Cuban	16,718	82	54	27	4.90	3.23	1.62
Central and South American	155,578	740	496	244	4.76	3.19	1.57
Other and unknown Hispanic	115,045	674	432	243	5.86	3.76	2.11

NOTES: Infant deaths are weighted so numbers may not exactly add to totals due to rounding. Neonatal is less than 28 days and postneonatal is 28 days to under 1 year. Race and Hispanic origin are reported separately on birth certificates. Race categories are consistent with the 1977 Office of Management and Budget standards. Persons of Hispanic origin may be of any race. In this table, Hispanic women are classified only by place of origin; non-Hispanic women are classified by race. See reference 2. Thirty states reported multiple-race data on the birth certificate for 2008 and 27 in 2007. The multiple-race data for these states were bridged to the single-race categories of the 1977 standards for comparability with other states; see references 2 and 3.

Table B. Infant, neonatal, and postneonatal mortality rates, by race and Hispanic origin of mother: United States, 1995 and 2000–2008 linked files

Race and Hispanic origin of mother	1995	2000	2001	2002	2003	2004	2005	2006	2007	2008	Percent change 2000 to 2008	Percent change 2007 to 2008
					Infant mortality rate							
All races	7.57	6.89	6.84	6.95	6.84	6.78	6.86	6.68	6.75	6.61	**4.1	**–2.1
Non-Hispanic white	6.28	5.70	5.72	5.80	5.70	5.66	5.76	5.58	5.63	5.52	**3.3	–2.0
Non-Hispanic black	14.65	13.59	13.46	13.89	13.60	13.60	13.63	13.35	13.31	12.67	**6.0	**–4.8
American Indian or Alaska Native	9.04	8.30	9.65	8.64	8.73	8.45	8.06	8.28	9.22	8.42	–1.4	–8.7
Asian or Pacific Islander	5.27	4.87	4.73	4.77	4.83	4.67	4.89	4.55	4.78	4.51	7.4	–5.6
Hispanic	6.27	5.59	5.44	5.62	5.65	5.55	5.62	5.41	5.51	5.59	0.0	1.5
Mexican	6.03	5.43	5.22	5.42	5.49	5.47	5.53	5.34	5.42	5.58	–2.8	3.0
Puerto Rican	8.88	8.21	8.53	8.20	8.18	7.82	8.30	8.01	7.71	7.29	11.2	–5.4
Cuban	5.29	4.54	4.28	3.72	4.57	4.55	4.42	5.08	5.18	4.90	–7.9	–5.4
Central and South American	5.52	4.64	4.98	5.06	5.04	4.65	4.68	4.52	4.57	4.76	–2.6	4.2
					Neonatal mortality rate							
All races	4.92	4.62	4.54	4.67	4.63	4.52	4.54	4.46	4.42	4.29	**–7.1	**–2.9
Non-Hispanic white	4.04	3.78	3.79	3.85	3.79	3.70	3.71	3.64	3.61	3.50	**–7.4	**–3.0
Non-Hispanic black	9.65	9.19	8.97	9.33	9.26	9.13	9.13	8.95	8.74	8.28	**–9.9	**–5.3
American Indian or Alaska Native	3.94	4.39	4.20	4.60	4.55	4.26	4.04	4.30	4.55	4.18	–4.8	–8.1
Asian or Pacific Islander	3.37	3.43	3.12	3.37	3.40	3.20	3.37	3.18	3.38	3.08	**–10.2	–8.9
Hispanic	4.13	3.77	3.64	3.83	3.92	3.83	3.86	3.74	3.72	3.76	–0.3	1.1
Mexican	3.94	3.61	3.49	3.64	3.76	3.74	3.78	3.73	3.68	3.78	4.7	2.7
Puerto Rican	6.11	5.80	5.99	5.81	5.70	5.34	5.95	5.44	5.14	4.98	**–14.1	–3.1
Cuban	3.61	3.20	2.50	3.23	3.36	2.81	3.05	3.60	3.65	3.23	0.9	–11.5
Central and South American	3.65	3.26	3.36	3.45	3.65	3.43	3.23	3.12	3.14	3.19	–2.1	1.6
					Postneonatal mortality rate							
All races	2.65	2.27	2.30	2.28	2.22	2.25	2.32	2.22	2.33	2.32	2.2	–0.4
Non-Hispanic white	2.23	1.92	1.93	1.95	1.91	1.96	2.05	1.94	2.02	2.02	**5.2	0.0
Non-Hispanic black	5.00	4.40	4.48	4.55	4.34	4.47	4.50	4.40	4.57	4.39	–0.2	–3.9
American Indian or Alaska Native	5.10	3.94	5.45	4.04	4.18	4.19	4.02	3.98	4.67	4.24	7.6	–9.2
Asian or Pacific Islander	1.90	1.44	1.61	1.40	1.43	1.47	1.51	1.37	1.40	1.43	–0.7	2.1
Hispanic	2.14	1.82	1.79	1.79	1.73	1.71	1.76	1.67	1.79	1.83	0.5	2.2
Mexican	2.09	1.82	1.73	1.78	1.73	1.73	1.75	1.61	1.75	1.80	–1.1	2.9
Puerto Rican	2.77	2.41	2.55	2.38	2.48	2.48	2.37	2.57	2.57	2.30	–4.6	–10.5
Cuban	1.68	*	1.71	*	*	1.74	1.37	1.42	1.53	1.62	- - -	5.9
Central and South American	1.86	1.38	1.61	1.60	1.39	1.22	1.46	1.41	1.43	1.57	13.8	9.8

** Significant at $p < 0.05$.

* Figure does not meet standards of reliability or precision; based on fewer than 20 deaths in the numerator.

- - - Data not available.

NOTES: Race and Hispanic origin are reported separately on birth certificates. Race categories are consistent with the 1977 Office of Management and Budget standards. Persons of Hispanic origin may be of any race. In this table, Hispanic women are classified only by place of origin; non-Hispanic women are classified by race. See reference 2. Thirty states reported multiple-race data on the birth certificate for 2008 and 27 in 2007. The multiple-race data for these states were bridged to the single-race categories of the 1977 standards for comparability with other states; see references 2 and 3.

highest rate, 12.67 per 1,000 live births, was for infants of non-Hispanic black mothers, 2.8 times greater than the lowest rate of 4.51 for infants of API mothers. Rates were also fairly high for infants of AIAN (8.42) and Puerto Rican (7.29) mothers. Rates were intermediate, but all below the U.S. rate, for infants of non-Hispanic white (5.52) and Mexican (5.58) mothers (Tables A and B). Cuban (4.90) and Central and South American (4.76) mothers also had low rates. These differences are explained in part by the differences in cause-specific infant mortality rates among race and Hispanic origin groups (12,13). Disparities in the infant mortality rate between non-Hispanic black and non-Hispanic white mothers by state are described and discussed in the sections, "Infant mortality by state" and "Disparities in the infant mortality rate by state."

Age at death

In 2008, nearly two-thirds (65 percent) of all infant deaths occurred during the neonatal period (from birth through age 27 days) (Table A). In 2008, the neonatal mortality rate was 4.29 deaths per 1,000 live births, 3 percent lower than in 2007 (4.42) (Figure 1). The 2008 postneonatal (aged 28 days to under 1 year) mortality rate of 2.32 was essentially unchanged from the previous year (14).

Non-Hispanic black women had the highest neonatal mortality rate of 8.28; the rate was 2.4 times that for non-Hispanic white women (3.50) (Figure 1). Neonatal mortality rates were also higher for Puerto Rican (4.98) and AIAN (4.18) women than for non-Hispanic white

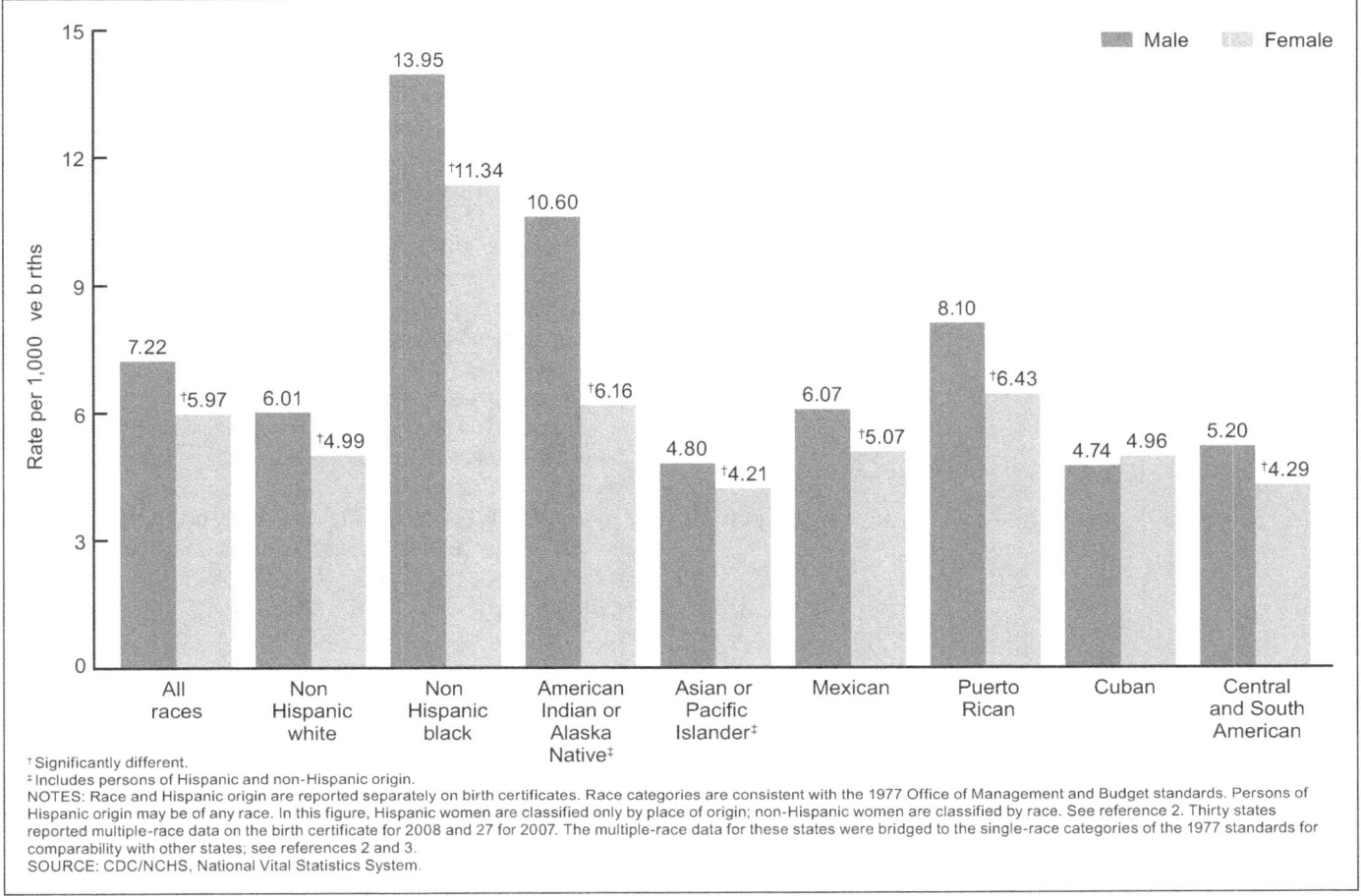

Figure 2. Infant mortality rates, by sex of child and race and ethnicity of mother: United States, 2008

women. Neonatal mortality rates were lower for API (3.08) and Central and South American (3.19) women than for non-Hispanic white women (Table A).

Infants of non-Hispanic black (4.39) and AIAN (4.24) women had the highest postneonatal mortality rates of any group—more than twice those for non-Hispanic white women (2.02) (Tables A and B). In contrast, postneonatal mortality rates for Mexican (1.80), API (1.43), Central and South American (1.57), and Cuban (1.62) women were 11–29 percent lower than for non-Hispanic white women (Table A).

From 2007 to 2008, neonatal mortality rates declined significantly for non-Hispanic white and non-Hispanic black women (Table B). Postneonatal rates for race and Hispanic origin groups were essentially unchanged from 2007 to 2008 (Table B).

The neonatal mortality rate declined 7 percent from 2000 (4.62) to 2008 (4.29). Declines in the neonatal mortality rate for this time period were significant for Puerto Rican (14 percent), non-Hispanic black (10 percent), API (10 percent), and non-Hispanic white (7 percent) mothers (Figure 1). Infants born to non-Hispanic white women were the only group with a decline in the postneonatal mortality rate from 2000 to 2008 (5 percent).

Infant mortality by state, and by race and ethnicity

To examine variations across states in more detail, and to obtain statistically reliable state-specific rates by race and Hispanic origin, 3 years of data were combined (Table 2). Across the United States, rates are generally higher in the South and Midwest and lower elsewhere. For 2006–2008, infant mortality rates ranged from a high of 10.16 for Mississippi to a low of 4.94 for Massachusetts and Utah. The highest rate noted (11.97) was for DC; however, the rate for DC is more appropriately compared with rates for other large U.S. cities, because of the high concentrations of high-risk women in these areas.

Infant mortality rates differ by state among race and Hispanic origin groups. Rates for infants of non-Hispanic black mothers could be reliably computed in 39 states and DC; among these states, mortality rates ranged from a high of 18.54 in Hawaii to a low of 7.66 in Washington. For infants of non-Hispanic white mothers, Alabama had the highest infant mortality rate (7.67) and New Jersey had the lowest (3.78). Among the 42 states where infant mortality rates could

Table C. Infant mortality rate, by state: United States, 2000, 2007, and 2008 linked files

[By place of residence]

State	Infant mortality rate per 1,000 live births			Number of infant deaths in 2008
	2000	2007	2008	
Total.	6.89	6.75	6.61	28,075
Alabama	9.51	9.94	9.47	611
Alaska.	6.92	6.61	6.03	69
Arizona	6.75	6.87	6.39	635
Arkansas	8.23	7.81	7.38	300
California	5.42	5.20	5.11	2,822
Colorado	6.14	6.13	6.21	435
Connecticut.	6.51	6.70	5.92	239
Delaware	9.59	7.64	8.35	101
District of Columbia . . .	12.13	12.97	11.17	102
Florida.	6.91	7.08	7.28	1,684
Georgia	8.45	8.01	7.99	1,171
Hawaii.	8.09	6.64	5.65	110
Idaho	7.56	6.83	5.73	144
Illinois	8.48	6.80	7.20	1,273
Indiana	7.79	7.58	6.84	607
Iowa.	6.43	5.48	5.69	229
Kansas	6.55	8.00	7.34	307
Kentucky	7.10	6.69	6.92	404
Louisiana	9.03	9.17	9.04	590
Maine	4.85	6.37	5.44	74
Maryland	7.51	8.02	7.96	615
Massachusetts	4.61	4.94	5.04	388
Michigan	8.19	7.94	7.40	896
Minnesota	5.62	5.56	5.92	429
Mississippi	10.64	9.98	9.95	447
Missouri.	7.19	7.42	7.14	578
Montana	6.02	6.27	7.15	90
Nebraska	7.18	6.76	5.48	148
Nevada	6.45	6.29	5.37	212
New Hampshire	5.82	5.43	3.87	53
New Jersey.	6.26	5.12	5.49	619
New Mexico	6.72	6.14	5.57	168
New York	6.40	5.56	5.52	1,381
North Carolina	8.60	8.52	8.25	1,079
North Dakota.	8.34	7.58	5.82	52
Ohio	7.66	7.77	7.70	1,146
Oklahoma.	8.40	8.41	7.19	394
Oregon	5.57	5.71	5.13	252
Pennsylvania.	7.10	7.53	7.38	1,101
Rhode Island.	6.24	7.27	5.89	71
South Carolina	8.77	8.51	8.05	508
South Dakota	5.22	6.28	8.28	100
Tennessee	9.11	8.30	8.16	698
Texas	5.60	6.30	6.17	2,501
Utah.	5.32	5.02	4.69	261
Vermont.	6.46	5.07	4.57	29
Virginia	6.91	7.73	6.88	734
Washington.	5.20	4.88	5.45	492
West Virginia	7.38	7.27	7.77	167
Wisconsin.	6.64	6.42	6.92	500
Wyoming	6.72	7.35	6.97	56
Guam	6.07	10.25	7.76	27
Puerto Rico.	9.60	8.43	8.42	384
Virgin Islands.	*	*	*	7

* Figure does not meet standards of reliability or precision; based on fewer than 20 deaths in the numerator.

be reliably computed (20 or more infant deaths) for Hispanic mothers, Pennsylvania had the highest rate (7.94) and Louisiana had the lowest (3.92).

For infants of AIAN mothers, mortality rates could be reliably computed for only 14 states, and for API mothers, rates could only be computed for 30 states. For infants of AIAN mothers, mortality rates ranged from 15.37 in North Carolina to 5.70 in New Mexico. Infant mortality rates for infants of API mothers ranged from 7.19 in Louisiana to 2.90 in New Jersey.

The data shown in Table 2 and summarized above illustrate wide disparities in infant mortality rates across states. One method for describing racial and ethnic disparities in infant mortality is to calculate the ratio between the infant mortality rates of two different racial and ethnic groups. The U.S. infant mortality rate ratio for non-Hispanic black relative to non-Hispanic white populations for the 3 years 2006–2008 was 2.35. It is important to keep in mind that large ratios can occur for two reasons: the infant mortality rate for non-Hispanic black women can be comparatively high, or the rate for non-Hispanic white women can be relatively low. The reverse can be true when the rate ratio is low. The rate ratio is not shown for several states that lack a calculable infant mortality rate for non-Hispanic black infants due to fewer than 20 infant deaths.

Areas with the highest rate ratios of 2.8 or greater for 2006–2008 were DC, Hawaii, New Jersey, and Wisconsin. Six areas had ratios less than 2.0: Alabama, Kentucky, Mississippi, Oklahoma, Oregon, and Washington (see Table 2 for rate ratios).

Sex of infant

In countries throughout the world, infant mortality rates are typically higher for male infants (15). In the United States in 2008, the overall infant mortality rate for male infants was 7.22 per thousand, 21 percent higher than the rate for female infants (5.97). Infant mortality rates were higher for male than female infants in each race and Hispanic-origin group (Table 1 and Figure 2), although the difference was not significant for infants of Cuban mothers.

Multiple births

For multiple births, the infant mortality rate was 28.73, five times the rate of 5.83 for singleton births (Table 1). Infant mortality rates for multiple births were higher than the rates for singleton births for all race and Hispanic-origin groups; rates for multiple births could not be reliably computed for Cuban mothers due to small numbers of events.

The risk of infant death increases with the increasing number of infants in the pregnancy. In 2008, the infant mortality rate for twins (27.33) was nearly 5 times, and the rate for triplets (59.70) was 10 times, the rate for single births (5.83) (tabular data not shown). Reliable infant mortality rates could not be computed for quadruplet and quintuplet and higher-order births due to small numbers of infant deaths in those categories. Infant mortality rates for twins and triplets in 2008 were not significantly different from the 2007 rates (14).

Multiple pregnancy can lead to an accentuation of maternal risks and complications associated with pregnancy (2,16–18). For example, multiple births are much more likely to be born preterm and at low birthweight than singleton births (2,16–18). The higher risk profile of multiple births has a substantial impact on overall infant mortality (17,19). For example, in 2008 multiple births accounted for 3 percent of all live births, but 15 percent of all infant deaths in the United States (Table 1).

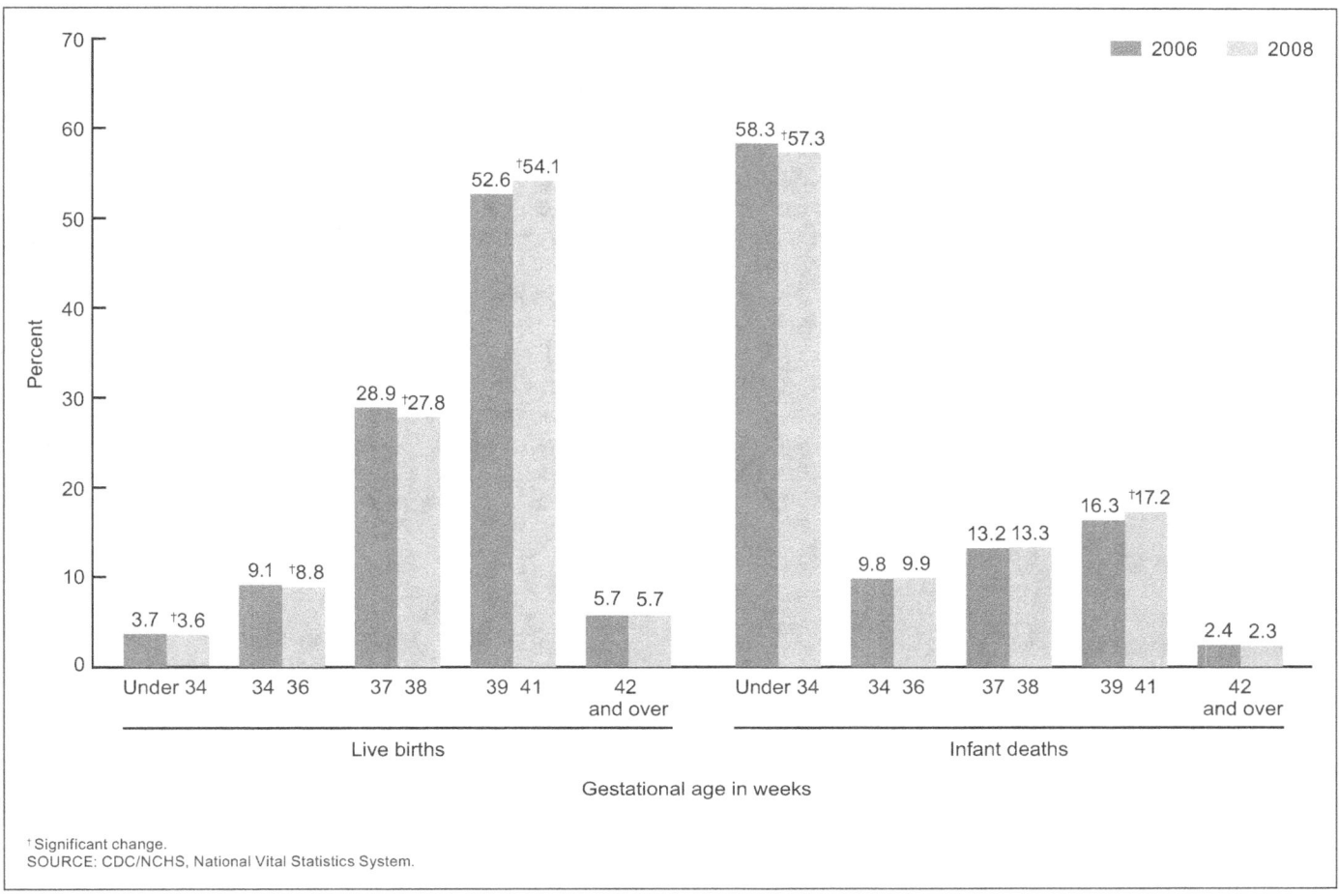

[†]Significant change.
SOURCE: CDC/NCHS, National Vital Statistics System.

Figure 3. Percent distribution of live births and infant deaths, by gestational age: United States, 2006 and 2008

Period of gestation

The gestational age of an infant is perhaps the most important predictor of his or her subsequent health and survival. Infants born too small and too soon have a much greater risk of death and both short- and long-term disability than those born at term (37–41 weeks of gestation) (20–24), and the percentage of preterm births has been linked to variations in infant mortality rates among countries (25). Because of their much greater risk of death, preterm infants have a large impact on the U.S. infant mortality rate. In 2008, more than two-thirds (67.2 percent) of all infant deaths occurred to the 12.3 percent of infants who were born preterm (Table 1). Infant mortality rates are highest for very preterm (under 32 weeks) infants, and the risk decreases sharply with increasing gestational age (20,24). In 2008, the infant mortality rate for very preterm infants (175.45) was 72 times the rate of 2.44 for term infants (Table 1). The infant mortality rate for infants born at 32–33 weeks of gestation was 17.58, seven times the rate for term infants.

Although mortality falls with increasing gestational age, even infants born only a few weeks early have a substantially increased risk of death and disability when compared with term infants (26–29). In 2008, the infant mortality rate for late preterm infants (34–36 weeks) was 7.40, three times the rate for infants born at term. Even within the

term period, infants born at 37–38 weeks of gestation (early term) had mortality rates that were 1.5 times higher than those born at 39–41 weeks of gestation (Table 1), leading some researchers to call for the prevention of early term births and the redefinition of "term" pregnancy (30,31).

Percentages of preterm births differed greatly by race and ethnicity; these differences have a large impact on infant mortality rates (12,14,32). In 2008, the percentage of preterm births ranged from 10.71 percent of births to API women to 17.54 percent of births to non-Hispanic black women (Table 3).

Gestational age-specific infant mortality rates also varied by race and ethnicity (Table 1). Compared with non-Hispanic white women, infant mortality rates were significantly higher for non-Hispanic black women for all gestational age categories except for 32–33 weeks of gestation. Infant mortality rates were higher for AIAN than for non-Hispanic white women at 37–41 weeks of gestation. In contrast, infant mortality rates were lower for API than for non-Hispanic white women for most gestational age groups except for under 32 weeks, while for Central and South American women, infant mortality rates were lower at under 32, 34–36, and 39–41 weeks of gestation. Patterns were mixed for Mexican and Puerto Rican women.

The percentage of preterm births increased by 36 percent, from 9.4 percent in 1984 to a high of 12.8 percent in 2006. However, since

2006, the trend has reversed, and the percentage preterm declined to 12.7 percent in 2007 and to 12.3 percent in 2008 (2). Figure 3 compares the gestational age distributions of live births and infant deaths for 2006 and 2008. The decline in the percentage of preterm births occurred during both the early (under 34 weeks) and late preterm periods. Early term (37–38 weeks) births also declined, while the percentage of births at 39–41 weeks of gestation increased. Similar to the changes for births, the percentage of infant deaths that were early preterm declined from 58.3 percent in 2006 to 57.3 percent in 2008, while the percentage of infant deaths to births at 39–41 weeks of gestation increased from 16.3 percent to 17.2 percent. Recent efforts to reduce "medically unnecessary" deliveries at under 39 weeks of gestation may have contributed to the recent decline in preterm and early term births (2,33–35).

The infant mortality rate at 32–33 weeks of gestation increased by 9 percent from 2007 (16.12) to 2008 (17.58), whereas changes in infant mortality rates from 2007 to 2008 were not statistically significant for the other gestational age groups (14). Thus, all of the decrease in the U.S. infant mortality rate from 2007 to 2008 can be accounted for by the decrease in preterm births (because gestational-age specific infant mortality rates did not decrease). This finding was supported by unpublished detailed analysis (data not shown).

Birthweight

Birthweight is another important predictor of infant health. It is closely associated with, but does not exactly correspond with, the period of gestation. Infant mortality rates are highest for the smallest infants and decrease sharply as birthweight increases. In 2008, infant mortality rates were 24 times higher for low birthweight (less than 2,500 grams) infants (54.53 per 1,000) than for infants with birthweights of 2,500 grams or more (2.29) (Table 1). The infant mortality rate for very low birthweight (less than 1,500 grams) infants was 237.39, more than 100 times the rate for infants with birthweights of 2,500 grams or more. Among the smallest infants [less than 500 grams (1 pound, 1 ounce or less)] (Table 4), 87 percent were reported to have died within the first year of life. Reporting of deaths among these very small infants may be incomplete (36). Infant mortality rates were lowest at birthweights of 3,500–4,499 grams.

Because of their much higher mortality rates, infants born at the lowest birthweights have a substantial impact on overall infant mortality rates. For example, infants born weighing less than 1,000 grams accounted for only 0.7 percent of births but nearly one-half (46.9 percent) of all infant deaths in the United States in 2008 (Table 4). Conversely, 91.8 percent of infants born in the United States in 2008 weighed 2,500 grams or more, but these infants accounted for less than one-third (32.0 percent) of infant deaths. The large race and Hispanic-origin variations in the percentage of births at low birthweight (less than 2,500 grams) (from 6.50 percent for Mexican women to 13.76 percent for non-Hispanic black women) mean that some racial and ethnic groups are disproportionately impacted by the high infant mortality rates for low birthweight infants (Table 3).

From 2000 to 2008, infant mortality rates for the total population declined for detailed birthweight categories between 500–1,249 grams and 2,000–3,999 grams (37) (Table 4). Changes for other detailed birthweight categories were not statistically significant.

Maternal age

Infant mortality rates vary with maternal age. In 2008, infants of teen mothers (9.59) and mothers aged 40 and over (8.07) had the highest rates. The lowest rates were for infants of mothers in their late 20s and early 30s (Table 1).

In 2008, among births to teenagers, infants of the youngest mothers (under age 15) had the highest mortality rate (14.92); the rate was 14.53 in 2007. The rate for infants of mothers aged 15–17 was 10.33 in 2008, similar to 2007 (10.27); the rate for infants of mothers aged 18–19 was 9.15 in 2008 compared with 9.49 in 2007 (tabular data not shown). The rate for infants of mothers aged 20–24 was 7.52 in 2008 compared with 7.67 in 2007 (14).

Infant mortality rates for births to non-Hispanic white mothers under age 20 were higher than for mothers aged 40 and over. In contrast, for Mexican mothers, rates for births to the oldest mothers were higher than rates for infants of teenagers.

Live-birth order

Infant mortality rates were generally higher for first births than for second births, and then generally increased as birth order increased (Table 1). In 2008, the infant mortality rate for first births (6.65) was 16 percent higher than for second births (5.74). The higher parities and, therefore, the highest-order births (fifth child and higher) are more likely to be associated with older maternal age, multiple births, and lower socioeconomic status (38).

Marital status

Marital status may be a marker for the presence or absence of social, emotional, and financial resources (39,40). Infants of mothers who are not married have been shown to be at higher risk for poor outcomes (41). In 2008, infants of unmarried mothers had an infant mortality rate of 8.87 per 1,000, 75 percent higher than the rate for infants of married mothers (5.06) (Table 1). Within each race and Hispanic origin group, infants of unmarried mothers had higher rates of mortality and, with the exception of Cuban infants, these differences were significant.

Nativity

In 2008, the infant mortality rate for mothers born in the 50 states and DC (6.99 per 1,000) was 38 percent higher than the rate for mothers born elsewhere (5.05) (Table 1). Among race and Hispanic origin groups, mothers born in the 50 states and DC had higher infant mortality rates than mothers born elsewhere for non-Hispanic white, non-Hispanic black, API, and Mexican mothers (Table 1).

A variety of hypotheses have been advanced to account for the lower infant mortality rate among infants of mothers born outside the 50 states and DC, including possible differences in migration selectivity, social support, and risk behaviors (42,43). Also, women born outside the 50 states and DC have been shown to have different characteristics than their U.S.-born counterparts with regard to socioeconomic and educational status (44).

Leading causes of infant death

Infant mortality rates for the five leading causes of infant death are presented in Table 5 by race and Hispanic origin of mother. The leading cause of infant death in the United States in 2008 was Congenital malformations, deformations and chromosomal abnormalities (congenital malformations), accounting for 20 percent of all infant deaths. Disorders relating to short gestation and low birthweight, not elsewhere classified (low birthweight) was second, accounting for 17 percent of all infant deaths, followed by Sudden infant death syndrome (SIDS), accounting for 8 percent of infant deaths. The fourth and fifth leading causes in 2008 were Newborn affected by maternal complications of pregnancy (maternal complications) (6 percent) and Accidents (unintentional injuries) (5 percent). Together the five leading causes accounted for 57 percent of all infant deaths in the United States in 2008. The order of the top five leading causes was the same as in 2007 and 2006. Infant mortality rates did not change significantly from 2007 to 2008 for any of the five leading causes of death.

In 2008, as in previous years, the rank order of leading causes of infant death varied substantially by race and Hispanic origin of the mother. Congenital malformations was the leading cause of infant death for all groups except for non-Hispanic black and Puerto Rican women, for whom low birthweight was the leading cause.

When differences between cause-specific infant mortality rates were examined by race and ethnicity, infant mortality rates from Congenital malformations were 24 percent higher for non-Hispanic black and Mexican women, and 16 percent higher for Central and South American than for non-Hispanic white women.

Infants of non-Hispanic black women had the highest mortality rates from low birthweight. The rate for non-Hispanic black women was nearly three times the rate for non-Hispanic white women. The rate for Puerto Rican women was more than twice the rate for non-Hispanic white women. The infant mortality rate from low birthweight was 16 percent higher for Mexican than for non-Hispanic white women.

Compared with non-Hispanic white women, SIDS rates were 66 percent higher for AIAN women and 95 percent higher for non-Hispanic black women (Figure 4). As most SIDS deaths occur during the postneonatal period, the high SIDS rates for infants of non-Hispanic black and AIAN women accounted for much of their elevated risk of postneonatal mortality. Compared with non-Hispanic white women, SIDS rates were 48 percent to 58 percent lower for Mexican, API, and Central and South American women.

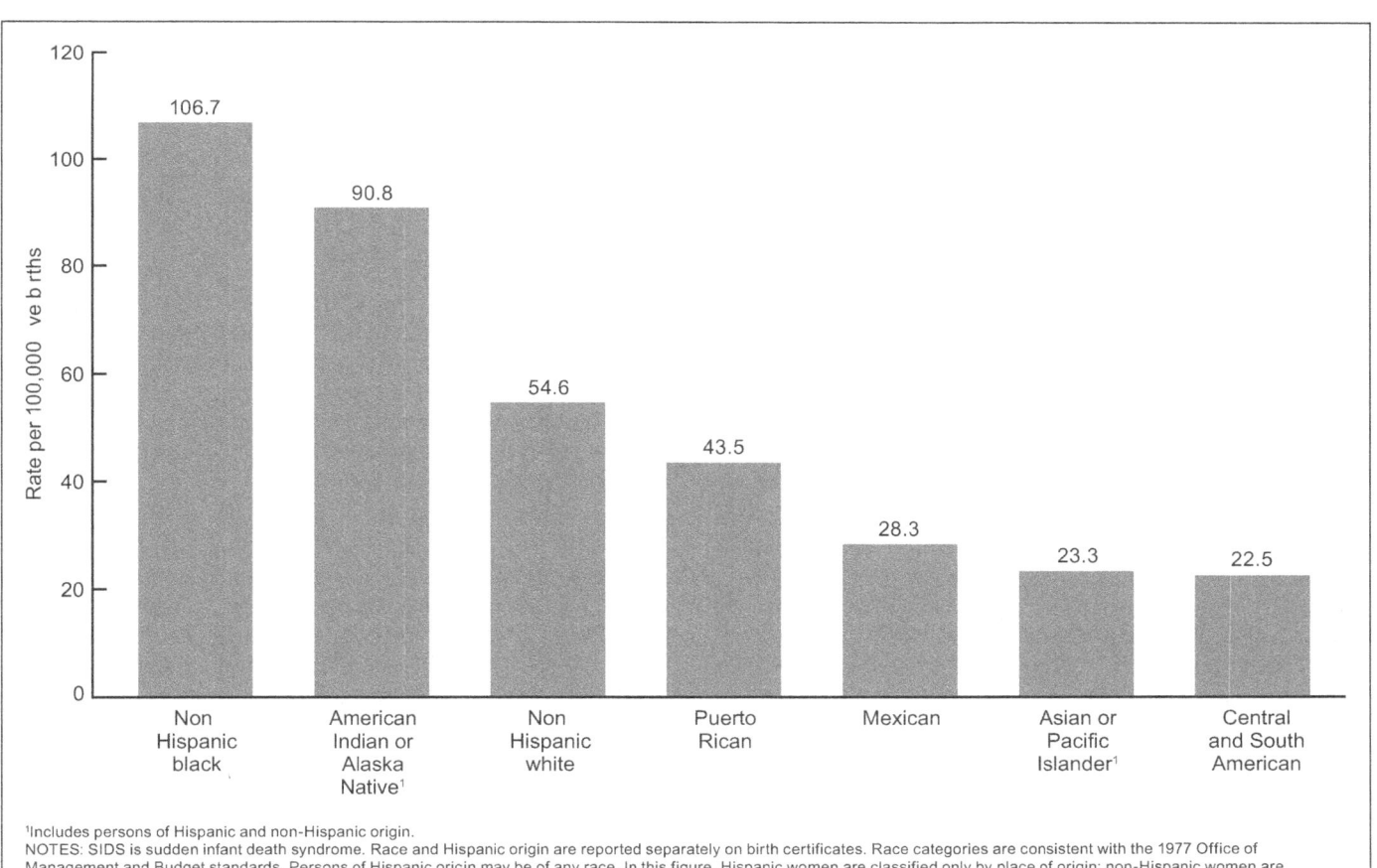

[1]Includes persons of Hispanic and non-Hispanic origin.
NOTES: SIDS is sudden infant death syndrome. Race and Hispanic origin are reported separately on birth certificates. Race categories are consistent with the 1977 Office of Management and Budget standards. Persons of Hispanic origin may be of any race. In this figure, Hispanic women are classified only by place of origin; non-Hispanic women are classified by race. See reference 2. Thirty states reported multiple-race data on the birth certificate for 2008 and 27 for 2007. The multiple-race data for these states were bridged to the single-race categories of the 1977 standards for comparability with other states; see references 2 and 3.
SOURCE: CDC/NCHS, National Vital Statistics System.

Figure 4. Infant mortality rates from SIDS, by race and Hispanic origin of mother: United States, 2008

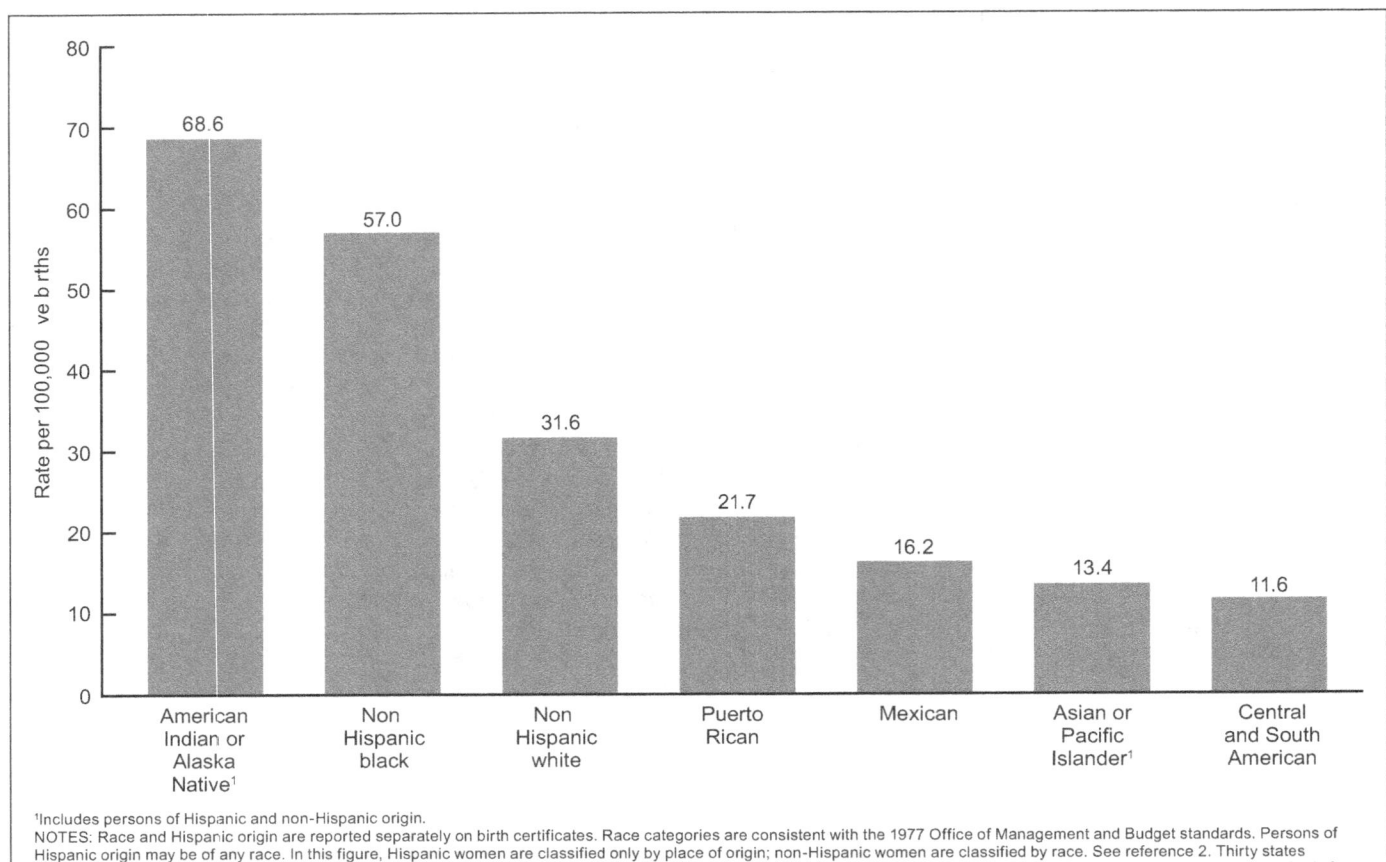

Figure 5. Infant mortality rates from unintentional injuries, by race and Hispanic origin of mother: United States, 2008

For maternal complications (including incompetent cervix, premature rupture of membranes, and multiple pregnancy, for example), infants of non-Hispanic black women had the highest mortality rates— 2.6 times those for non-Hispanic white women. Non-Hispanic black women have a much higher percentage of preterm births (Table 3), which may help to explain the high infant mortality rates from maternal complications, as this cause occurs predominantly among preterm infants. Infant mortality rates from maternal complications were 37 percent lower for Central and South American than for non-Hispanic white women.

The infant mortality rate from unintentional injuries was 2.2 times higher for AIAN women than the rate for non-Hispanic white women (Figure 5). For non-Hispanic black women, the rate from unintentional injuries was 80 percent higher than for non-Hispanic white women. Infant mortality rates from unintentional injuries were 49 percent to 58 percent lower for Mexican and for API women than for non-Hispanic white women.

Preterm-related causes of death

To more fully assess the impact of preterm birth on infant mortality, CDC researchers have developed a grouping of *preterm-related* causes of death. A cause of death was considered preterm-related if 75 percent or more of infants whose deaths were attributed to that cause were born at under 37 weeks of gestation, and the cause of death was a direct consequence of preterm birth based on a clinical evaluation and review of the literature (45,46).

The preterm-related cause-of-death grouping includes Disorders related to short gestation and low birthweight not elsewhere classified, and most of the Maternal complications of pregnancy category from the five leading causes of death. Also included are a variety of other causes of death closely associated with prematurity such as Respiratory distress of newborn, Bacterial sepsis of newborn, Necrotizing enterocolitis of newborn, and others. The comprehensive list of preterm-related cause-of-death categories (ICD–10 codes) is shown in the note on Table 6. Even this comprehensive grouping probably underestimates the total impact of preterm-related infant mortality, as some cause-of-death categories (notably those beginning with the words "Other" and "All other") had a high percentage of preterm infant deaths but lacked sufficient specificity to be able to establish the etiologic connection to prematurity with any degree of certainty.

Table 6 shows trends in preterm-related infant mortality by race and Hispanic origin of mother from 2000 to 2008. In 2008, 9,952 out of a total of 28,075 infant deaths (35.4 percent) in the United States were preterm-related. The percentage of infant deaths that were preterm-related increased from 34.6 percent in 2000 to a high of 36.1 percent in 2006; however, since 2006, the percentage of infant deaths that were preterm-related, declined to 35.4 percent in 2008.

The impact of preterm-related infant deaths varied considerably by maternal race and ethnicity. In 2008, 44 percent of infant deaths to both non-Hispanic black and Puerto Rican women were due to preterm-related causes, while the percentage was somewhat lower for other racial and ethnic groups (Table 6).

Preterm-related infant mortality rates varied considerably by race and ethnicity of the mother (Table 6). The preterm-related infant mortality rate was more than three times higher for non-Hispanic black (5.56) than for non-Hispanic white (1.69) women. The preterm-related infant mortality rate was 91 percent higher for Puerto Rican women (3.22), and 12 percent higher for Mexican (1.90) than for non-Hispanic white women. For Central and South American women, the preterm-related infant mortality rate (1.47) was 13 percent lower than for non-Hispanic white women.

From 2007 to 2008, preterm-related infant mortality rates declined by 4 percent for the total population, by 5 percent for non-Hispanic white women, and by 7 percent for non-Hispanic black women. In contrast, preterm-related infant mortality rates increased by 11 percent for Mexican women. Changes for other racial and ethnic groups were not statistically significant.

Preterm-related infant mortality explains much of the higher risk of infant mortality for non-Hispanic black and Puerto Rican women, when compared with white women. In 2008, 86 percent of the difference in the overall infant mortality rates between Puerto Rican and non-Hispanic white women was due to preterm-related causes of death. About 54 percent of the difference between non-Hispanic black and non-Hispanic white women was due to these causes. In contrast, for AIAN women, preterm-related infant mortality only explained 9 percent of their elevated infant mortality rate when compared with non-Hispanic white women. Other causes of death such as SIDS and unintentional injuries explained a larger part of the infant mortality difference between AIAN and non-Hispanic white women (13).

References

1. National Center for Health Statistics. Public use data file documentation: 2008 period linked birth/infant death data set. Available from: http://www.cdc.gov/nchs/data_access/VitalStatsOnline.htm.
2. Martin JA, Hamilton BE, Sutton PD, et al. Births: Final data for 2008. National vital statistics reports; vol 59 no 1. Hyattsville, MD: National Center for Health Statistics. 2010.
3. National Center for Health Statistics. User guide to the 2008 natality public use file. Available from: ftp://ftp.cdc.gov/pub/Health_Statistics/NCHS/Dataset_Documentation/DVS/natality/UserGuide2008.pdf.
4. Miniño AM, Murphy SL, Xu JQ, Kochanek KD. Deaths: Final data for 2008. National vital statistics reports; vol 59 no 10. Hyattsville, MD: National Center for Health Statistics. 2011.
5. World Health Organization. International statistical classification of diseases and related health problems, tenth revision. Geneva: World Health Organization. 1992.
6. Osterman MJK, Martin JA, Mathews TJ, Hamilton BE. Expanded data from the new birth certificate, 2008. National vital statistics reports; vol 59 no 7. Hyattsville, MD: National Center for Health Statistics. 2011.
7. Rosenberg HM, Maurer JD, Sorlie PD, et al. Quality of death rates by race and Hispanic origin: A summary of current research, 1999.
National Center for Health Statistics. Vital Health Stat 2(128). 1999.
8. National Center for Health Statistics. U.S. Standard Certificate of Live Birth. 2003. Available from: http://www.cdc.gov/nchs/data/dvs/birth11-03final-ACC.pdf.
9. Hamilton BE, Ventura SJ. Characteristics of births to single- and multi-race women: California, Hawaii, Pennsylvania, Utah, and Washington, 2003. National vital statistics reports; vol 55 no 15. Hyattsville, MD: National Center for Health Statistics. 2007.
10. Tomashek KM, Qin C, Hsia J, Iyasu S, Barfield WD, Flowers LM. Infant mortality trends and differences between American Indian/Alaska Native infants and white infants in the United States, 1989–1991 and 1998–2000. Am J Public Health 96(12):2222–7. 2006.
11. Singh GK, Kogan MD. Persistent socioeconomic disparities in infant, neonatal, and postneonatal mortality rates in the United States, 1969–2001. Pediatrics 119(4):e928–39. 2007.
12. MacDorman MF. Race and ethnic disparities in fetal mortality, preterm birth, and infant mortality in the United States: An overview. Semin Perinatol 35(4):200–8. 2011.
13. MacDorman MF, Mathews TJ. Understanding racial and ethnic disparities in U.S. infant mortality rates. NCHS data brief, no 74. Hyattsville, MD: National Center for Health Statistics. 2011.
14. Mathews TJ, MacDorman MF. Infant mortality statistics from the 2007 period linked birth/infant death data set. National vital statistics reports; vol 59 no 6. Hyattsville, MD: National Center for Health Statistics. 2011.
15. Fuse K, Crenshaw EM. Gender imbalance in infant mortality: A cross-national study of social structure and female infanticide. Soc Sci Med 62(2):360–74. 2005.
16. Martin JA, Hamilton BE, Osterman MJK. Three decades of twin births in the United States, 1980–2009. NCHS data brief, no 80. Hyattsville, MD: National Center for Health Statistics. 2012.
17. American College of Obstetricians and Gynecologists. Multiple gestation: Complicated twin, triplet, and high order multifetal pregnancy. ACOG Practice Bulletin, no 56. Washington, DC: American College of Obstetricians and Gynecologists. 2004.
18. Goldenberg RL, Culhane JF, Iams JD, Romero R. Epidemiology and causes of preterm birth. Lancet 371(9606):75–84. 2008.
19. Luke B, Brown MB. The changing risk of infant mortality by gestation, plurality, and race: 1989–1991 versus 1999–2001. Pediatrics 118(6):2488–97. 2006.
20. Saigal S, Doyle LW. An overview of mortality and sequelae of preterm birth from infancy to adulthood. Lancet 371(9608):261–9. 2008.
21. Hintz SR, Kendrick DE, Wilson-Costello DE, Das A, Bell EF, Vohr BR, et al. Early childhood neurodevelopmental outcomes are not improving for infants born at <25 weeks' gestational age. Pediatrics 127(1):62–70. 2011.
22. Loe IM, Lee ES, Luna B, Feldman HM. Behavior problems of 9–16 year old preterm children: Biological, sociodemographic, and intellectual contributions. Early Hum Dev 87(4):247–52. 2011.
23. O'Shea TM, Allred EN, Dammann O, Hirtz D, Kuban KC, Paneth N, et al. The ELGAN study of the brain and related disorders in extremely low gestational age newborns. Early Hum Dev 85(11):719–25. 2009.
24. Stoll BJ, Hansen NI, Bell EF, Shankaran S, Laptook AR, Walsh MC, et al. Neonatal outcomes of extremely preterm infants from the NICHD Neonatal Research Network. Pediatrics 126(3):443–56. 2010.
25. MacDorman MF, Mathews TJ. Behind international rankings of infant mortality: How the United States compares with Europe. NCHS data brief, no 23. Hyattsville, MD: National Center for Health Statistics. 2009.
26. Teune MJ, Bakhuizen S, Gyamfi Bannerman C, Opmeer BC, van Kaam AH, van Wassenaer AG, et al. A systematic review of severe morbidity in infants born late preterm. Am J Obstet Gynecol 205(4):374.e1–9. 2011.

27. Talge NM, Holzman D, Wang J, Lucia V, Gardiner J, Breslau N. Late-preterm birth and its association with cognitive and socioemotional outcomes at 6 years of age. Pediatrics 126(6):1124–31. 2010.

28. Woythaler MA, McCormick MC, Smith VC. Late preterm infants have worse 24-month neurodevelopmental outcomes than term infants. Pediatrics 127(3):e622–9. 2011.

29. Cheng YW, Kaimal AJ, Bruckner TA, Halloran DR, Caughey AB. Perinatal morbidity associated with late preterm deliveries compared with deliveries between 37 and 40 weeks of gestation. BJOG 188(12):1446–54. 2011.

30. Clark SL, Fleischman AR. Term pregnancy: Time for a redefinition. Clin Perinatol 38(3):557–64. 2011.

31. Fleischman AR, Oinuma M, Clark SL. Rethinking the definition of "term pregnancy." Obstet Gynecol 116(1):136–9. 2010.

32. Culhane JF, Goldenberg RL. Racial disparities in preterm birth. Semin Perinatol 35(4):234–9. 2011.

33. Clark SL, Frye DR, Meyers JA, Belfort MA, Dildy GA, Kofford S, et al. Reduction in elective delivery at <39 weeks of gestation: Comparative effectiveness of 3 approaches to change and the impact on neonatal intensive care admission and stillbirth. Am J Obstet Gynecol 203(5):449.e1–6. 2010.

34. Oshiro BT, Henry E, Wilson J, Branch DW, Varner MW. Decreasing elective deliveries before 39 weeks of gestation in an integrated health care system. Obstet Gynecol 113(4):804–11. 2009.

35. Martin JA, Osterman MJK, Sutton PD. Are preterm births on the decline in the United States? Recent data from the National Vital Statistics System. NCHS data brief, no 39. Hyattsville, MD: National Center for Health Statistics. 2010.

36. Paulson J, Ramsini W, Conrey E, et al. Unregistered deaths among extremely low birthweight infants—Ohio, 2006. MMWR 56(42):1101–3. 2007.

37. Mathews TJ, Menacker F, MacDorman MF. Infant mortality statistics from the 2000 period linked birth/infant death data set. National vital statistics reports; vol 50 no 12. Hyattsville, MD: National Center for Health Statistics. 2002.

38. Bai J, Wong FW, Bauman A, Mohsin M. Parity and pregnancy outcomes. Am J Obstet Gynecol 186(2): 274–8. 2002.

39. McNamara TK, Orav EJ, Wilkins-Haug L, Chang G. Social support and prenatal alcohol use. J Womens Health 15(1):70–6. 2006.

40. Feldman PJ, Dunkel-Schetter C, Sandman CA, Wadhwa PD. Maternal social support predicts birth weight and fetal growth in human pregnancy. Psychosom Med 62(5):715–25. 2000.

41. Raatikainen K, Heiskanen N, Heinonen S. Marriage still protects pregnancy. BJOG 112(10):1411–6. 2005.

42. Singh GK, Miller BA. Health, life expectancy, and mortality patterns among immigrant populations in the United States. Can J Public Health 95(3):I14–21. 2004.

43. Liu KL, Laraque F. Higher mortality rate among infants of US-born mothers compared to foreign-born mothers in New York City. J Immigr Minor Health 8(3):281–9. 2006.

44. Acevedo-Garcia D, Soobader M, Berkman LF. The differential effect of foreign-born status on low birth weight by race/ethnicity and education. Pediatrics 115(1):20–30. 2005.

45. Callaghan WM, MacDorman MF, Rasmussen SA, Qin C, Lackritz EM. The contribution of preterm birth to infant mortality rates in the United States. Pediatrics 118(4):1566–73. 2006.

46. MacDorman MF, Callaghan WM, Mathews TJ, Hoyert DL, Kochanek KD. Trends in preterm-related infant mortality by race and ethnicity, United States, 1999–2004. Int J Health Serv 37(4):635–41. 2007.

47. Buehler JW, Prager K, Hogue CJ. The role of linked birth and infant death certificates in maternal and child health epidemiology in the United States. Am J Prev Med 19(1 Suppl):3–11. 2000.

48. National Center for Health Statistics. 2003 revision of the U.S. Standard Certificate of Live Birth. Available from: http://www.cdc.gov/nchs/nvss/vital_certificate_revisions.htm. 2003.

49. National Center for Health Statistics. Report of the Panel to Evaluate the U.S. Standard Certificates. Available from: http://www.cdc.gov/nchs/data/dvs/panelreport_acc.pdf. 2000.

50. National Center for Health Statistics. Technical appendix. Vital statistics of the United States, 2003, vol I natality. Hyattsville, MD. Available from: http://www.cdc.gov/nchs/data/TechApp03_1-09.pdf.

51. Martin JA, Hamilton BE, Sutton PD, et al. Births: Final data for 2007. National vital statistics reports; vol 58 no 24. Hyattsville, MD: National Center for Health Statistics. 2010.

52. Office of Management and Budget. Race and ethnic standards for federal statistics and administrative reporting. Statistical Policy Directive 15. May 12, 1977.

53. Office of Management and Budget. Revisions to the standards for the classification of federal data on race and ethnicity. Fed Reg 62FR58781–58790. October 30, 1997. Available from: http://www.whitehouse.gov/omb/fedreg_1997standards.

54. Johnson DP. Coding and editing multiple race and ethnicity. 2004 joint meeting of NAPHSIS and VSCP. Portland, OR. 2004. Available from: http://www.naphsis.org/index.asp?downloadid=75.

55. National Center for Health Statistics. Vital statistics, instructions for classifying the underlying cause of death. NCHS instruction manual; part 2a. Hyattsville, MD. Published annually.

56. National Center for Health Statistics. Vital statistics, instructions for classifying multiple causes of death. NCHS instruction manual; part 2b. Hyattsville, MD. Published annually.

57. Israel RA, Rosenberg HM, Curtin LR. Analytical potential for multiple cause-of-death data. Am J Epidemiol 124(2): 161–79. 1986.

58. National Center for Health Statistics. 2008 documentation initial release: Mortality multiple cause-of-death public use record. Hyattsville, MD. Available from: http://www.cdc.gov/nchs/data/dvs/Record_Layout_2008.pdf [Accessed 2/23/12].

59. World Health Organization. Manual of the International Statistical Classification of Diseases, Injuries, and Causes of Death, Ninth Revision. Geneva: World Health Organization. 1977.

60. Anderson RN, Miniño AM, Hoyert DL, Rosenberg HM. Comparability of cause of death between ICD–9 and ICD–10: Preliminary estimates. National vital statistics reports; vol 49 no 2. Hyattsville, MD: National Center for Health Statistics. 2001.

61. National Center for Health Statistics. Comparability of cause-of-death between ICD revisions. 2008. Available from: http://www.cdc.gov/nchs/nvss/mortality/comparability_icd.htm.

62. National Center for Health Statistics. ICD–10 cause-of-death lists for tabulating mortality statistics. NCHS instruction manual; part 9. Hyattsville, MD. 1999.

63. Brillinger DR. The natural variability of vital rates and associated statistics. Biometrics 42(4):693–734. 1986.

List of Detailed Tables

1. Infant mortality rates, live births, and infant deaths, by selected characteristics and by race and Hispanic origin of mother: United States, 2008 linked file   14
2. Infant mortality rates, by race and Hispanic origin of mother: United States and each state, Puerto Rico, Virgin Islands, and Guam, 2006–2008 linked files   17
3. Percentage of live births with selected maternal and infant characteristics, by race and Hispanic origin of mother: United States, 2008 linked file   18
4. Live births, infant, neonatal, and postneonatal deaths and mortality rates, by race and Hispanic origin of mother and birthweight: United States, 2008 linked file, and percent change in birthweight-specific infant mortality, 2000–2008 linked file   19
5. Infant deaths and mortality rates for the five leading causes of infant death, by race and Hispanic origin of mother: United States, 2008 linked file   21
6. Number and percentage of preterm-related infant deaths, and preterm-related infant mortality rates, by race and Hispanic origin of mother: United States, 2000–2008 linked files   22

Table 1. Infant mortality rates, live births, and infant deaths, by selected characteristics and by race and Hispanic origin of mother: United States, 2008 linked file

Characteristics	All races and origins[1]	Non-Hispanic		American Indian or Alaska Native[2]	Asian or Pacific Islander	Hispanic		Puerto Rican	Cuban	Central and South American
		White	Black			Total[1]	Mexican			
				Infant mortality rates per 1,000 live births in specified group						
Total.	6.61	5.52	12.67	8.42	4.51	5.59	5.58	7.29	4.90	4.76
Age at death										
Total neonatal	4.29	3.50	8.28	4.18	3.08	3.76	3.78	4.98	3.23	3.19
Early neonatal (under 7 days)	3.45	2.78	6.67	3.35	2.52	3.03	3.07	4.12	2.39	2.51
Late neonatal (7–27 days)	0.85	0.72	1.61	0.83	0.56	0.73	0.70	0.87	*	0.68
Postneonatal.	2.32	2.02	4.39	4.24	1.43	1.83	1.80	2.30	1.62	1.57
Sex										
Male	7.22	6.01	13.95	10.60	4.80	6.08	6.07	8.10	4.74	5.20
Female	5.97	4.99	11.34	6.16	4.21	5.08	5.07	6.43	4.96	4.29
Plurality										
Single births	5.83	4.79	11.13	7.99	4.13	5.07	5.11	6.09	4.28	4.29
Plural births	28.73	23.58	51.93	25.43	16.59	27.55	27.34	44.57	*	22.76
Birthweight										
Less than 2,500 grams	54.53	47.71	69.60	57.32	38.71	55.00	58.13	57.21	41.98	48.33
Less than 1,500 grams	237.39	216.71	262.73	230.77	210.85	242.87	256.07	247.03	170.12	211.88
1,500–2,499 grams.	14.31	14.36	14.16	20.13	9.96	15.36	16.72	10.42	*	14.66
2,500 grams or more.	2.29	2.20	3.53	4.38	1.44	1.88	1.92	1.82	1.69	1.61
Period of gestation										
Less than 37 weeks	35.76	30.82	53.91	32.27	28.14	30.71	31.68	38.27	22.44	25.66
Less than 32 weeks	175.45	160.26	208.27	147.42	161.85	162.87	171.58	179.18	118.84	138.62
32–33 weeks	17.58	18.33	19.24	*	10.19	15.89	16.52	*	*	14.62
34–36 weeks	7.40	7.57	8.75	9.17	5.64	6.20	6.79	4.20	*	5.10
37–41 weeks	2.44	2.29	3.72	4.58	1.68	2.10	2.10	2.14	2.13	1.91
37–38 weeks	3.13	3.04	4.35	5.57	2.15	2.65	2.56	2.94	*	2.58
39–41 weeks	2.08	1.93	3.34	4.08	1.43	1.81	1.86	1.72	*	1.56
42 weeks or more	2.69	2.53	4.63	*	*	2.18	2.26	*	*	*
Age of mother										
Under 20 years	9.59	9.03	13.79	10.18	8.53	7.01	6.82	8.46	*	6.48
20–24 years	7.52	6.66	12.70	8.81	5.54	5.49	5.37	7.26	*	5.05
25–29 years	5.90	4.88	11.87	8.78	4.10	5.11	4.97	7.67	*	4.34
30–34 years	5.16	4.27	11.62	5.72	3.99	4.81	5.00	5.39	*	4.07
35–39 years	6.19	5.06	14.04	*	4.54	6.07	6.48	6.99	*	4.73
40–54 years	8.07	6.68	15.25	*	5.61	8.61	9.19	*	*	7.04
Live-birth order										
1.	6.65	5.50	13.12	6.96	4.46	5.85	5.99	7.43	4.09	4.59
2.	5.74	4.89	11.20	9.00	3.77	5.02	4.95	6.72	5.12	4.45
3.	6.35	5.53	11.45	9.37	5.31	5.06	5.02	5.79	*	4.36
4.	7.71	6.78	13.52	10.22	5.71	5.89	5.84	7.03	*	5.87
5 or more	10.16	8.36	16.89	8.10	7.90	7.95	7.61	14.35	*	7.14
Marital status										
Married.	5.06	4.54	10.53	5.85	4.05	5.11	5.27	6.43	3.75	4.14
Unmarried	8.87	7.94	13.49	9.75	6.79	6.03	5.87	7.76	6.22	5.32
Mother's place of birth										
Born in the 50 states and DC	6.99	5.55	13.08	8.46	5.56	6.24	6.19	7.09	5.42	5.40
Born elsewhere	5.05	4.08	8.60	7.42	4.17	5.09	5.16	7.87	4.22	4.63

See footnotes at end of table.

Table 1. Infant mortality rates, live births, and infant deaths, by selected characteristics and by race and Hispanic origin of mother: United States, 2008 linked file—Con.

Characteristics	All races and crigins[1]	Non-Hispanic White	Non-Hispanic Black	American Indian or Alaska Native[2]	Asian or Pacific Islander	Hispanic Total[1]	Hispanic Mexican	Hispanic Puerto Rican	Hispanic Cuban	Hispanic Central and South American
					Live births					
Total.	4,247,726	2,267,817	623,031	49,537	253,184	1,041,239	684,883	69,015	16,718	155,578
Sex										
Male	2,173,409	1,162,622	316,447	25,196	130,590	531,999	349,495	35,435	8,647	79,591
Female	2,074,317	1,105,195	306,584	24,341	122,594	509,240	335,388	33,580	8,071	75,987
Plurality										
Single births	4,102,795	2,180,421	599,538	48,318	245,469	1,017,139	670,436	66,861	16,131	151,667
Plural births	144,931	87,396	23,493	1,219	7,715	24,100	14,447	2,154	587	3,911
Birthweight										
Less than 2,500 grams	348,543	164,088	85,709	3,681	20,742	72,624	44,541	6,817	1,310	10,448
Less than 1,500 grams	62,843	27,045	19,115	650	2,969	12,653	7,705	1,348	241	1,784
1,500–2,499 grams.	285,700	137,043	66,594	3,031	17,773	59,971	36,836	5,469	1,069	8,664
2,500 grams or more.	3,898,189	2,103,288	537,214	45,847	232,396	968,541	640,318	62,189	15,408	145,095
Not stated	994	441	108	9	46	74	24	9	*	35
Period of gestation										
Less than 37 weeks	523,040	252,337	109,127	6,724	27,077	125,805	79,855	9,720	2,273	18,627
Less than 32 weeks	84,230	36,229	23,907	1,065	3,806	18,696	11,470	1,825	345	2,698
32–33 weeks	66,648	31,255	15,127	860	3,237	15,918	10,049	1,233	283	2,394
34–36 weeks	372,162	184,853	70,093	4,799	20,034	91,191	58,336	6,662	1,645	13,535
37–41 weeks	3,478,057	1,883,722	480,048	39,285	213,997	851,072	562,069	55,064	13,607	127,459
37–38 weeks	1,181,269	618,355	181,350	13,293	73,097	292,059	190,212	19,032	5,287	43,058
39–41 weeks	2,296,788	1,265,367	298,698	25,992	140,900	559,013	371,857	36,032	8,320	84,401
42 weeks or more	240,795	129,433	32,856	3,447	11,743	62,859	41,956	4,146	832	9,265
Not stated	5,834	2,325	1,000	81	367	1,503	1,003	85	6	227
Age of mother										
Under 20 years	440,525	169,788	106,690	8,941	7,618	147,240	101,164	11,934	1,307	13,115
20–24 years	1,052,191	511,758	198,117	16,801	31,038	293,054	196,763	21,502	3,963	36,653
25–29 years	1,195,781	670,814	156,473	12,649	71,220	281,319	184,831	17,607	4,114	45,130
30–34 years	956,723	562,032	98,062	7,166	85,537	199,984	128,163	11,317	4,201	36,597
35–39 years	488,880	287,453	50,506	3,210	47,616	97,235	60,475	5,438	2,566	19,252
40–54 years	113,626	65,972	13,183	770	10,155	22,407	13,487	1,217	567	4,831
Live-birth order										
1.	1,703,924	952,478	244,342	17,670	115,331	368,783	228,158	28,143	7,817	58,212
2.	1,330,542	740,746	174,211	13,337	88,494	310,332	200,675	20,524	5,865	49,667
3.	705,118	354,166	105,085	8,753	31,243	204,475	142,244	11,737	2,094	28,241
4.	291,351	130,565	50,876	4,894	10,329	94,109	68,271	4,977	602	11,584
5 or more	190,189	78,318	41,981	4,568	6,454	58,131	42,457	3,276	268	6,866
Not stated	26,602	11,544	6,536	315	1,333	5,409	3,078	358	72	1,008
Marital status										
Married.	2,521,134	1,617,796	172,483	16,930	210,352	494,023	333,632	24,424	9,321	74,176
Unmarried	1,726,592	650,021	450,548	32,607	42,832	547,216	351,251	44,591	7,397	81,402
Mother's place of birth										
Born in the 50 states and DC	3,198,446	2,125,759	540,395	46,078	51,092	422,306	260,273	50,052	7,939	21,653
Born elsewhere	1,034,416	136,848	78,183	3,370	200,554	616,747	423,788	18,428	8,768	133,587
Not stated	14,864	5,210	4,453	89	1,538	2,186	822	535	11	338

See footnotes at end of table.

Table 1. Infant mortality rates, live births, and infant deaths, by selected characteristics and by race and Hispanic origin of mother: United States, 2008 linked file—Con.

Characteristics	All races and origins[1]	Non-Hispanic White	Non-Hispanic Black	American Indian or Alaska Native[2]	Asian or Pacific Islander	Hispanic Total[1]	Mexican	Puerto Rican	Cuban	Central and South American
					Infant deaths					
Total.	28,075	12,509	7,894	417	1,143	5,821	3,822	503	82	740
Age at death										
Total neonatal	18,238	7,936	5,158	207	780	3,915	2,588	344	54	497
Early neonatal (under 7 days)	14,648	6,310	4,157	166	639	3,159	2,106	284	40	391
Late neonatal (7–27 days)	3,590	1,626	1,001	41	141	756	482	60	14	106
Postneonatal.	9,837	4,573	2,735	210	363	1,906	1,234	159	27	244
Sex										
Male	15,689	6,993	4,416	267	627	3,234	2,121	287	41	414
Female	12,386	5,516	3,478	150	516	2,587	1,701	216	40	326
Plurality										
Single births	23,911	10,448	6,674	386	1,015	5,157	3,427	407	69	651
Plural births	4,164	2,061	1,220	31	128	664	395	96	13	89
Birthweight										
Less than 2,500 grams	19,007	7,829	5,965	211	803	3,994	2,589	390	55	505
Less than 1,500 grams	14,918	5,861	5,022	150	626	3,073	1,973	333	41	378
1,500–2,499 grams.	4,089	1,968	943	61	177	921	616	57	14	127
2,500 grams or more.	8,935	4,629	1,894	201	335	1,823	1,230	113	26	234
Not stated	134	51	34	4	5	4	2	*	*	1
Period of gestation										
Less than 37 weeks	18,703	7,778	5,883	217	762	3,863	2,530	372	51	478
Less than 32 weeks	14,778	5,806	4,979	157	616	3,045	1,968	327	41	374
32–33 weeks	1,172	573	291	16	33	253	166	17	3	35
34–36 weeks	2,753	1,399	613	44	113	565	396	28	7	69
37–41 weeks	8,470	4,314	1,788	180	359	1,789	1,178	118	29	243
37–38 weeks	3,693	1,877	789	74	157	775	487	56	17	111
39–41 weeks	4,777	2,436	999	106	202	1,014	691	62	12	132
42 weeks or more	648	328	152	15	12	137	95	10	1	14
Not stated	255	90	72	5	10	32	18	2	*	5
Age of mother										
Under 20 years	4,225	1,533	1,471	91	65	1,032	690	101	13	85
20–24 years	7,914	3,410	2,516	148	172	1,608	1,056	156	19	185
25–29 years	7,055	3,271	1,858	111	292	1,437	918	135	17	196
30–34 years	4,938	2,399	1,139	41	341	961	641	61	8	149
35–39 years	3,027	1,455	709	17	216	590	392	38	16	91
40–54 years	917	441	201	8	57	193	124	12	8	34
Live-birth order										
1.	11,333	5,237	3,205	123	514	2,158	1,367	209	32	267
2.	7,634	3,620	1,951	120	334	1,558	993	138	30	221
3.	4,479	1,957	1,203	82	166	1,034	714	68	13	123
4.	2,247	885	688	50	59	554	399	35	3	68
5 or more	1,933	655	709	37	51	462	323	47	2	49
Not stated	449	156	137	4	19	55	27	5	1	13
Marital status										
Married.	12,765	7,348	1,817	99	852	2,524	1,759	157	35	307
Unmarried	15,310	5,161	6,077	318	291	3,297	2,062	346	46	433
Mother's place of birth										
Born in the 50 states and DC	22,348	11,802	7,067	390	284	2,634	1,610	355	43	117
Born elsewhere	5,228	558	672	25	836	3,140	2,186	145	37	618
Not stated	500	148	154	1	24	48	25	3	1	5

* Figure does not meet standards of reliability or precision; based on fewer than 20 deaths in the numerator.

[1]Includes other and unknown Hispanic and origin not stated, not shown separately.

[2]Includes Aleuts and Eskimos.

NOTES: DC is District of Columbia. Infant deaths are weighted so numbers may not exactly add to totals due to rounding. Not stated responses were included in totals but not distributed among groups for rate computations. Race and Hispanic origin are reported separately on birth certificates. Race categories are consistent with the 1977 Office of Management and Budget standards. Persons of Hispanic origin may be of any race. In this table Hispanic women are classified only by place of origin; non-Hispanic women are classified by race. See reference 2. Thirty states reported multiple-race data on the birth certificate for 2008 and 27 in 2007. The multiple-race data for these states were bridged to the single-race categories of the 1977 standards for comparability with other states; see references 2 and 3.

Table 2. Infant mortality rates, by race and Hispanic origin of mother: United States and each state, Puerto Rico, Virgin Islands, and Guam, 2006–2008 linked files

[By place of residence]

Area	Total	Race and Hispanic origin of mother					Ratio of rate, non-Hispanic black and non-Hispanic white
		Non-Hispanic white	Non-Hispanic black	American Indian or Alaska Native[1]	Asian or Pacific Islander	Hispanic	
		Infant mortality rates per 1,000 live births in specified group					
United States[2]	6.68	5.58	13.11	8.65	4.62	5.50	2.35
Alabama	9.47	7.67	13.73	*	*	7.50	1.79
Alaska	6.54	4.10	*	12.24	*	*	*
Arizona	6.54	6.04	14.85	7.57	6.54	6.13	2.46
Arkansas	7.89	6.70	13.53	*	*	5.71	2.02
California	5.12	4.51	10.72	7.05	4.30	4.88	2.38
Colorado	6.04	5.13	11.97	*	4.90	6.96	2.33
Connecticut	6.27	4.80	13.11	*	5.73	6.35	2.73
Delaware	8.03	5.89	13.46	*	*	7.10	2.29
District of Columbia	11.97	4.46	17.68	*	*	*	3.96
Florida	7.21	5.71	12.83	*	5.75	5.38	2.25
Georgia	8.02	5.87	12.70	*	4.37	5.06	2.16
Hawaii	6.04	4.58	18.54	*	6.27	4.98	4.05
Idaho	6.46	5.95	*	*	*	7.91	*
Illinois	7.10	5.70	13.45	*	5.31	5.91	2.36
Indiana	7.44	6.47	15.36	*	*	6.28	2.37
Iowa	5.43	5.06	11.10	*	*	6.61	2.19
Kansas	7.50	6.94	14.62	*	5.36	7.15	2.11
Kentucky	7.04	6.62	12.13	*	*	5.07	1.83
Louisiana	9.38	6.62	13.88	*	7.19	3.92	2.10
Maine	6.04	5.90	*	*	*	*	*
Maryland	7.98	5.50	12.98	*	5.33	5.33	2.36
Massachusetts	4.94	4.04	10.90	*	3.06	6.08	2.70
Michigan	7.56	5.87	14.70	*	4.89	7.09	2.50
Minnesota	5.55	4.77	11.33	10.25	5.65	4.64	2.38
Mississippi	10.16	7.07	13.82	*	*	6.64	1.95
Missouri	7.34	6.18	14.49	*	4.02	5.12	2.34
Montana	6.47	5.89	*	9.22	*	*	*
Nebraska	5.93	5.33	12.98	*	*	5.21	2.44
Nevada	6.10	5.29	12.54	*	4.96	5.69	2.37
New Hampshire	5.10	5.00	*	*	*	*	*
New Jersey	5.35	3.78	12.06	*	2.90	5.12	3.19
New Mexico	5.81	6.12	*	5.70	*	5.60	*
New York	5.57	4.29	11.29	*	3.35	5.01	2.63
North Carolina	8.29	6.17	14.62	15.37	5.62	6.32	2.37
North Dakota	6.44	5.63	*	12.27	*	*	*
Ohio	7.74	6.25	15.03	*	4.59	6.88	2.40
Oklahoma	7.85	7.52	13.91	8.36	5.64	5.09	1.85
Oregon	5.41	5.22	10.16	9.34	4.78	5.36	1.95
Pennsylvania	7.52	5.78	14.04	*	6.06	7.94	2.43
Rhode Island	6.47	4.28	10.56	*	*	7.77	2.47
South Carolina	8.30	6.04	12.97	*	5.32	5.87	2.15
South Dakota	7.15	5.59	*	13.00	*	*	*
Tennessee	8.37	6.54	15.36	*	5.78	6.47	2.35
Texas	6.22	5.48	11.69	7.47	4.16	5.61	2.13
Utah	4.94	4.73	*	*	7.10	5.03	*
Vermont	5.12	4.95	*	*	*	*	*
Virginia	7.24	5.48	13.40	*	4.74	5.97	2.45
Washington	5.01	4.33	7.66	9.15	4.26	5.28	1.77
West Virginia	7.38	7.11	14.93	*	*	*	2.10
Wisconsin	8.57	5.37	15.14	9.92	6.84	6.34	2.82
Wyoming	7.05	6.32	*	*	*	7.90	*
Puerto Rico	8.49	- - -	- - -	- - -	- - -	- - -	- - -
Virgin Islands	5.03	*	*	*	*	*	*
Guam	10.56	*	*	*	11.11	*	*

* Figure does not meet standards of reliability or precision; based on fewer than 20 deaths in the numerator. ·

- - - Data not available.

[1] Includes Aleuts and Eskimos.

[2] Excludes data for Puerto Rico, Virgin Islands, and Guam.

NOTES: Race categories are consistent with the 1977 Office of Management and Budget standards. Persons of Hispanic origin may be of any race. In this table, Hispanic women are classified only by place of origin; non-Hispanic women are classified by race. See reference 2. Thirty states reported multiple-race data on the birth certificate for 2008 and 27 for 2007. The multiple-race data for these states were bridged to the single-race categories of the 1977 standards for comparability with other states; see references 2 and 3.

Table 3. Percentage of live births with selected maternal and infant characteristics, by race and Hispanic origin of mother: United States, 2008 linked file

Characteristic	All races and origins[1]	Non-Hispanic				Hispanic				
		White	Black	American Indian or Alaska Native[2]	Asian or Pacific Islander	Total[1]	Mexican	Puerto Rican	Cuban	Central and South American
Birthweight:										
Less than 1,500 grams	1.48	1.19	3.07	1.31	1.17	1.22	1.13	1.95	1.44	1.15
Less than 2,500 grams	8.21	7.24	13.76	7.43	8.19	6.98	6.50	9.88	7.84	6.72
Preterm births[3]	12.33	11.14	17.54	13.60	10.71	12.10	11.68	14.10	13.60	11.99
Births to mothers under age 20	10.5	7.5	17.3	18.0	3.0	14.2	14.9	17.2	8.2	9.0
Fourth and higher-order births	11.4	9.3	15.1	19.2	6.7	14.7	16.2	12.0	5.2	11.9
Births to unmarried mothers.	39.7	27.8	71.6	65.8	16.9	51.3	50.1	63.4	41.8	52.7
Mothers born in the 50 states and DC . .	75.6	94.0	87.4	93.2	20.3	40.6	38.0	73.1	47.5	13.9

[1]Includes other and unknown Hispanic and origin not stated not shown separately.

[2]Includes Aleuts and Eskimos.

[3]Born prior to 37 completed weeks of gestation.

NOTES: DC is District of Columbia. Race and Hispanic origin are reported separately on birth certificates. Race categories are consistent with 1977 Office of Management and Budget standards. Persons of Hispanic origin may be of any race. In this table, Hispanic women are classified only by place of origin; non-Hispanic women are classified by race. See reference 2. Thirty states reported multiple-race data on the birth certificate for 2008 and 27 for 2007. The multiple-race data for these states were bridged to the single-race categories of the 1977 standards for comparability with other states; see references 2 and 3.

Table 4. Live births, infant, neonatal, and postneonatal deaths and mortality rates, by race and Hispanic origin of mother and birthweight: United States, 2008 linked file, and percent change in birthweight-specific infant mortality, 2000–2008 linked file

Race, and birthweight in grams	Number in 2008				Mortality rate per 1,000 live births in 2008			Percent change in infant mortality rate 2000–2008
	Live births	Infant deaths	Neonatal deaths	Postneonatal deaths	Infant	Neonatal	Postneonatal	
All races and origins	4,247,726	28,075	18,238	9,837	6.61	4.29	2.32	**–4.1
Less than 2,500	348,543	19,007	15,206	3,801	54.53	43.63	10.91	**–8.2
Less than 1,500	62,843	14,918	12,890	2,029	237.39	205.11	32.29	**–2.8
Less than 500	7,225	6,276	6,103	173	868.65	844.71	23.94	2.7
500–749	11,282	5,071	4,264	807	449.48	377.95	71.53	**–5.6
750–999	12,330	1,771	1,288	484	143.63	104.46	39.25	**–7.8
1,000–1,249	14,465	1,007	678	329	69.62	46.87	22.74	**–10.0
1,250–1,499	17,541	793	557	236	45.21	31.75	13.45	–0.8
1,500–1,999	67,232	1,842	1,193	649	27.40	17.74	9.65	–3.1
2,000–2,499	218,468	2,246	1,123	1,124	10.28	5.14	5.14	**–12.4
2,500 or more	3,898,189	8,935	2,904	6,031	2.29	0.74	1.55	**–7.3
2,500–2,999	788,641	3,311	1,229	2,082	4.20	1.56	2.64	**–8.1
3,000–3,499	1,564,369	3,443	1,023	2,421	2.07	0.61	1.45	**–13.0
3,500–3,999	1,121,186	1,680	470	1,210	1.50	0.42	1.08	**–10.2
4,000–4,499	280,415	382	123	260	1.36	0.44	0.93	–7.5
4,500–4,999	39,131	89	42	47	2.27	1.07	1.20	10.7
5,000 or more	4,447	28	17	11	6.30	*	*	2.9
Not stated	994	134	129	5	. . .	. . .	. . .	. . .
Non-Hispanic white	2,267,817	12,509	7,936	4,573	5.52	3.50	2.02	**–3.2
Less than 2,500	164,088	7,828	6,331	1,498	47.71	38.58	9.13	**–9.7
Less than 1,500	27,045	5,861	5,168	693	216.71	191.09	25.62	**–5.6
Less than 500	2,596	2,293	2,237	57	883.28	861.71	21.96	2.7
500–749	4,427	2,001	1,750	251	452.00	395.30	56.70	**–8.1
750–999	5,241	762	583	179	145.39	111.24	34.15	–8.6
1,000–1,249	6,471	440	321	119	68.00	49.61	18.39	**–15.9
1,250–1,499	8,310	364	278	87	43.80	33.45	10.47	1.3
1,500–1,999	32,539	858	596	262	26.37	18.32	8.05	–2.0
2,000–2,499	104,504	1,109	566	543	10.61	5.42	5.20	**–11.2
2,500 or more	2,103,288	4,629	1,555	3,074	2.20	0.74	1.46	–3.9
2,500–2,999	368,735	1,658	644	1,013	4.50	1.75	2.75	–2.6
3,000–3,499	866,124	1,790	538	1,252	2.07	0.62	1.45	**–9.2
3,500–3,999	662,053	907	266	641	1.37	0.40	0.97	**–10.5
4,000–4,499	78,633	211	76	135	1.18	0.43	0.76	–13.2
4,500–4,999	25,143	52	24	27	2.07	0.95	1.07	16.9
5,000 or more	2,600	12	6	6	*	*	*	*
Not stated	441	51	49	2	. . .	. . .	. . .	. . .
Non-Hispanic black	623,031	7,894	5,159	2,735	12.67	8.28	4.39	**–6.8
Less than 2,500	85,709	5,965	4,627	1,338	69.60	53.98	15.61	**–7.9
Less than 1,500	19,115	5,022	4,184	838	262.73	218.89	43.84	–1.1
Less than 500	2,727	2,354	2,273	82	863.22	833.52	30.07	3.2
500–749	3,904	1,690	1,328	363	432.89	340.16	92.98	–4.9
750–999	3,786	505	321	184	133.39	84.79	48.60	–5.1
1,000–1,249	4,145	268	148	120	64.66	35.71	28.95	–10.4
1,250–1,499	4,553	204	115	90	44.81	25.26	19.77	0.8
1,500–1,999	16,225	428	225	204	26.38	13.87	12.57	–5.3
2,000–2,499	50,369	514	218	296	10.20	4.33	5.88	**–13.3
2,500 or more	537,214	1,894	497	1,397	3.53	0.93	2.60	**–10.6
2,500–2,999	158,396	788	231	557	4.97	1.46	3.52	**–12.3
3,000–3,499	240,241	746	178	568	3.11	0.74	2.36	**–14.8
3,500–3,999	113,308	290	69	222	2.56	0.61	1.96	–10.5
4,000–4,499	21,903	53	10	43	2.42	*	1.96	0.8
4,500–4,999	2,963	12	6	6	*	*	*	*
5,000 or more	403	4	3	1	*	*	*	*
Not stated	108	34	34	–	. . .	. . .	. . .	. . .

See footnotes at end of table.

Table 4. Live births, infant, neonatal, and postneonatal deaths and mortality rates, by race and Hispanic origin of mother and birthweight: United States, 2008 linked file, and percent change in birthweight-specific infant mortality, 2000–2008 linked file—Con.

Race, and birthweight in grams	Number in 2008				Mortality rate per 1,000 live births in 2008			Percent change in infant mortality rate 2000–2008
	Live births	Infant deaths	Neonatal deaths	Postneonatal deaths	Infant	Neonatal	Postneonatal	
American Indian or Alaska Native[1]	49,537	417	207	210	8.42	4.18	4.24	1.4
Less than 2,500	3,681	211	159	53	57.32	43.19	14.40	−8.0
Less than 1,500	650	150	135	15	230.77	207.69	*	−13.6
Less than 500	66	56	56	–	848.48	848.48	*	−5.5
500–749	127	57	51	6	448.82	401.57	*	−1.3
750–999	130	23	19	4	176.92	*	*	−38.1
1,000–1,249	156	11	8	3	*	*	*	*
1,250–1,499	171	3	1	2	*	*	*	*
1,500–1,999	734	34	15	18	46.32	*	*	*
2,000–2,499	2,297	27	8	19	11.75	*	*	−24.9
2,500 or more	45,847	201	45	156	4.38	0.98	3.40	2.3
2,500–2,999	8,457	49	10	39	5.79	*	4.61	−5.9
3,000–3,499	18,660	83	18	65	4.45	*	3.48	−6.3
3,500–3,999	13,959	52	10	42	3.73	*	3.01	23.5
4,000–4,499	3,975	9	3	6	*	*	*	*
4,500–4,999	682	6	2	4	*	*	*	*
5,000 or more	114	2	2	–	*	*	*	*
Not stated	9	4	3	1	. . .	. . .	. . .	. . .
Asian or Pacific Islander	253,184	1,143	780	363	4.51	3.08	1.43	−7.4
Less than 2,500	20,742	803	652	151	38.71	31.43	7.28	**−12.9
Less than 1,500	2,969	626	547	78	210.85	184.24	26.27	−9.9
Less than 500	327	287	281	6	877.68	859.33	*	1.3
500–749	469	191	164	27	407.25	349.68	57.57	−11.1
750–999	579	65	46	19	112.26	79.45	*	−33.7
1,000–1,249	692	50	33	16	72.25	47.69	*	5.3
1,250–1,499	902	33	23	10	36.59	25.50	*	−48.3
1,500–1,999	3,794	79	51	28	20.82	13.44	7.38	−24.8
2,000–2,499	13,979	98	54	44	7.01	3.86	3.15	−15.0
2,500 or more	232,396	335	123	212	1.44	0.53	0.91	−12.2
2,500–2,999	59,034	129	52	77	2.19	0.88	1.30	−17.7
3,000–3,499	107,084	125	48	77	1.17	0.45	0.72	−4.1
3,500–3,999	54,352	65	17	47	1.20	*	0.86	−9.8
4,000–4,499	10,459	13	4	9	*	*	*	*
4,500–4,999	1,310	2	1	1	*	*	*	*
5,000 or more	157	1	1	–	*	*	*	*
Not stated	46	5	5	–	. . .	. . .	. . .	. . .
Hispanic	1,041,239	5,821	3,915	1,906	5.59	3.76	1.83	0.0
Less than 2,500	72,624	3,993	3,247	747	54.98	44.71	10.29	−2.1
Less than 1,500	12,653	3,073	2,677	396	242.87	211.57	31.30	3.1
Less than 500	1,388	1,179	1,150	29	849.42	828.53	20.89	3.3
500–749	2,277	1,073	919	154	471.23	403.60	67.63	−1.3
750–999	2,542	406	310	96	159.72	121.95	37.77	−2.4
1,000–1,249	2,928	234	164	70	79.92	56.01	23.91	5.9
1,250–1,499	3,518	181	133	47	51.45	37.81	13.36	4.7
1,500–1,999	13,608	435	302	132	31.97	22.19	9.70	−2.5
2,000–2,499	46,363	486	268	218	10.48	5.78	4.70	−9.4
2,500 or more	968,541	1,823	664	1,160	1.88	0.69	1.20	**−9.2
2,500–2,999	191,465	672	286	386	3.51	1.49	2.02	−8.1
3,000–3,499	428,035	678	230	447	1.58	0.54	1.04	**−18.6
3,500–3,999	274,454	356	105	251	1.30	0.38	0.91	−12.2
4,000–4,499	64,517	95	30	66	1.47	0.46	1.02	17.6
4,500–4,999	8,895	16	8	8	*	*	*	*
5,000 or more	1,175	7	5	2	*	*	*	*
Not stated	74	4	4	–	. . .	. . .	. . .	. . .

** Not significant at $p < 0.05$.

* Figure does not meet standards of reliability or precision; based on fewer than 20 deaths in the numerator.

. . . Category not applicable.

– Quantity zero.

[1]Includes Aleuts and Eskimos.

NOTES: Infant deaths are weighted so numbers may not exactly add to totals due to rounding. Neonatal is less than 28 days and postneonatal is 28 days to under 1 year. Race and Hispanic origin are reported separately on birth certificates. Race categories are consistent with the 1977 Office of Management and Budget standards. Persons of Hispanic origin may be of any race. In this table, Hispanic women are classified only by place of origin; non-Hispanic women are classified by race. See reference 2. Thirty states reported multiple-race data on the birth certificate for 2008 and 27 for 2007. The multiple-race data for these states were bridged to the single-race categories of the 1977 standards for comparability with other states; see references 2 and 3.

Table 5. Infant deaths and mortality rates for the five leading causes of infant death, by race and Hispanic origin of mother: United States, 2008 linked file

[Rates per 100,000 live births in specified group]

Cause of death (based on International Classification of Diseases, Tenth Revision, 1992)	All races			Non–Hispanic white			Non–Hispanic black			American Indian or Alaska Native[1]			Asian or Pacific Islander[2]		
	Rank	Number	Rate	Rank	Number	Rate	Rank	Number	Rate	Rank	Number	Rate	Rank	Number	Rate
All causes	...	28,075	660.9	...	12,509	551.6	...	7,894	1,267.0	...	417	841.8	...	1,143	451.5
Congenital malformations, deformations, and chromosomal abnormalities (Q00–Q99)	1	5,681	133.7	1	2,820	124.3	2	962	154.4	1	75	151.4	1	250	98.7
Disorders related to short gestation and low birth weight, not elsewhere classified (P07)	2	4,757	112.0	2	1,712	75.5	1	1,768	283.8	3	44	88.8	2	211	83.3
Sudden infant death syndrome (R95)	3	2,350	55.3	3	1,238	54.6	3	665	106.7	2	45	90.8	4	59	23.3
Newborn affected by maternal complications of pregnancy (P01)	4	1,775	41.8	4	766	33.8	4	546	87.6	6	14	*	3	78	30.8
Accidents (unintentional injuries) (V01–X59)	5	1,314	30.9	5	716	31.6	5	355	57.0	4	34	68.6	6	34	13.4

Cause of death (based on International Classification of Diseases, Tenth Revision, 1992)	Total Hispanic[3]			Mexican[4]			Puerto Rican[5]			Central and South American[6]		
	Rank	Number	Rate	Rank	Number	Rate	Rank	Number	Rate	Rank	Number	Rate
All causes	...	5,821	559.0	...	3,822	558.1	...	503	728.8	...	740	475.6
Congenital malformations, deformations, and chromosomal abnormalities (Q00–Q99)	1	1,523	146.3	1	1,055	154.0	2	75	108.7	1	224	144.0
Disorders related to short gestation and low birth weight, not elsewhere classified (P07)	2	939	90.2	2	600	87.6	1	114	165.2	2	121	77.8
Sudden infant death syndrome (R95)	4	328	31.5	4	194	28.3	3	30	43.5	3	35	22.5
Newborn affected by maternal complications of pregnancy (P01)	3	347	33.3	3	253	36.9	4	24	34.8	4	33	21.2
Accidents (unintentional injuries) (V01–X59)	7	171	16.4	6	111	16.2	7	15	*	8	18	*

... Category not applicable.

* Figure does not meet standards of reliability or precision; based on fewer than 20 deaths in the numerator.

[1]For American Indian or Alaska Native women, Newborn affected by complications of placenta, cord and membranes (P02) was the fifth leading cause of death with 20 deaths and a rate of 40.4.

[2]For Asian or Pacific Islander women, Newborn affected by complications of placenta, cord and membranes was the fifth leading cause of death with 41 deaths and a rate of 16.2.

[3]For Hispanic women, Newborn affected by complications of placenta, cord and membranes (P02) was the fifth leading cause of death with 198 deaths and a rate of 19.0.

[4]For Mexican women, Newborn affected by complications of placenta, cord and membranes (P02) was the fifth leading cause of death with 135 deaths and a rate of 19.7.

[5]For Puerto Rican women, Respiratory distress of newborn (P22) was tied for the fourth leading cause of death with 24 deaths and a rate of 34.8.

[6]For Central and South American women, Diseases of the circulatory system (I00–I99), Infections specific to the perinatal period (P35–P39) and Bacterial sepsis of newborn (P36) were tied for the fifth leading cause of death, each with 24 deaths and a rate of 15.4.

NOTE: Reliable cause-specific infant mortality rates cannot be computed for Cuban women because of the small number of infant deaths (86). Race and Hispanic origin are reported separately on birth certificates. Race categories are consistent with the 1977 Office of Management and Budget standards. Persons of Hispanic origin may be of any race. In this table, Hispanic women are classified only by place of origin; non-Hispanic women are classified by race. See reference 2. Thirty states reported multiple-race data on the birth certificate for 2008 and 27 for 2007. The multiple-race data for these states were bridged to the single-race categories of the 1977 standards for comparability with other states; see references 2 and 3.

Table 6. Number and percentage of preterm-related infant deaths, and preterm-related infant mortality rates, by race and Hispanic origin of mother: United States, 2000–2008 linked files

Year	All races and origins	Non-Hispanic white	Non-Hispanic black	American Indian or Alaska native	Asian or Pacific Islander	Total Hispanic[1]	Mexican	Puerto Rican	Central and South American
			Number of preterm-related infant deaths						
2008.	9,952	3,843	3,466	97	418	2,009	1,303	222	229
2007.	10,498	4,104	3,755	111	430	1,956	1,276	208	269
2006.	10,303	4,134	3,709	100	358	1,868	1,229	221	252
2005.	10,364	4,206	3,655	86	401	1,880	1,266	218	241
2004.	10,180	4,171	3,641	83	378	1,752	1,192	195	238
2003.	10,331	4,358	3,615	91	364	1,761	1,163	200	256
2002.	9,965	4,342	3,581	90	321	1,540	1,018	190	192
2001.	9,767	4,289	3,561	79	280	1,436	951	196	189
2000.	9,673	4,141	3,586	96	298	1,411	929	189	170
			Percent of total infant deaths that are preterm-related						
2008.	35.4	30.7	43.9	23.3	36.6	34.5	34.1	44.1	30.9
2007.	36.0	31.6	45.0	24.3	35.4	33.4	32.6	39.4	34.6
2006.	36.1	32.1	45.0	25.3	32.6	33.2	32.0	41.2	33.7
2005.	36.5	32.0	45.9	23.8	35.5	34.0	33.0	41.4	34.0
2004.	36.5	32.1	46.3	22.4	35.3	33.4	32.2	40.7	35.7
2003.	36.9	32.9	46.1	24.2	34.1	34.2	32.4	41.8	37.4
2002.	35.6	32.6	44.6	24.6	31.9	31.3	29.9	40.3	30.1
2001.	35.5	32.2	44.9	19.6	29.6	31.0	29.8	39.9	31.3
2000.	34.6	30.8	43.7	27.7	30.5	30.9	29.4	39.6	32.3
			Preterm-related infant mortality rate[2]						
2008.	2.34	1.69	5.56	1.96	1.65	1.93	1.90	3.22	1.47
2007.	2.43	1.78	5.99	2.25	1.69	1.84	1.77	3.04	1.58
2006.	2.42	1.79	6.01	2.10	1.49	1.80	1.71	3.30	1.52
2005.	2.50	1.84	6.26	1.92	1.74	1.91	1.83	3.44	1.59
2004.	2.48	1.82	6.29	1.89	1.65	1.85	1.76	3.19	1.66
2003.	2.53	1.88	6.28	2.11	1.65	1.93	1.78	3.42	1.89
2002.	2.48	1.89	6.19	2.12	1.52	1.76	1.62	3.31	1.52
2001.	2.43	1.84	6.04	1.89	1.40	1.69	1.56	3.40	1.56
2000.	2.38	1.75	5.93	2.30	1.49	1.73	1.60	3.25	1.50

[1]Includes Cuban and other and unknown Hispanic. Cuban data were not shown separately because of small numbers of infant deaths.

[2]Rate per 1,000 live births in specified group.

NOTES: Preterm-related deaths are those where the infant was born preterm (before 37 completed weeks of gestation) with the underlying cause of death assigned to one of the following ICD–10 categories: K550, P000, P010, P011, P015, P020, P021, P027, P070–P073, P102, P220–229, P250–279, P280, P281, P360–369, P520–523, or P77. Race and Hispanic origin are reported separately on birth certificates. Race categories are consistent with the 1977 Office of Management and Budget standards. Persons of Hispanic origin may be of any race. In this table, Hispanic women are classified only by place of origin; non-Hispanic women are classified by race. See reference 2. Thirty states reported multiple-race data on the birth certificate for 2007 and 27 in 2007. The multiple-race data for these states were bridged to the single-race categories of the 1977 standards for comparability with other states; see references 2 and 3.

Technical Notes

Differences between period and cohort data

From 1983 through 1991, the Centers for Disease Control and Prevention's National Center for Health Statistics (NCHS) produced linked files in a birth cohort format (47). Beginning with 1995 data, linked files are produced first using a period format and then subsequently using a birth cohort format. The 2008 period linked file contains a numerator file that consists of all infant deaths occurring in 2008 that have been linked to their corresponding birth certificates, whether the birth occurred in 2007 or in 2008. In contrast, the 2008 birth cohort linked file will contain a numerator file that consists of all infant deaths to babies born in 2008 whether the death occurred in 2008 or 2009. Beginning with 1995 data, the period linked file is the basis for all official NCHS linked file statistics.

Weighting

In 2008, a record weight was added to the linked file to compensate for the 1.3 percent of infant death records that could not be linked to their corresponding birth certificates. This procedure was initiated in 1995. Records for Puerto Rico, the Virgin Islands, and Guam were not weighted. The percentage of records linked varied by registration area (from 95.0 percent to 100.0 percent with all but three areas—Louisiana, Texas, and Utah—at 97.5 percent or higher) (Table I). The number of infant deaths in the linked file for the 50 states and the District of Columbia (DC) was weighted to equal the sum of the linked plus unlinked infant deaths by state of occurrence of birth and age of death (under age 7 days, 7–27 days, and 28 days to under 1 year). The addition of the weight reduced the potential for bias in comparing infant mortality rates by characteristics.

The 2008 linked file started with 28,107 infant death records. Of these records, 27,748 were linked; 359 were unlinked because corresponding birth certificates could not be identified. The 28,107 linked and unlinked records contained 32 records of infants whose mothers' usual place of residence was outside of the United States. These 32 records were excluded to derive a weighted total of 28,075 infant deaths for 2008.

Comparison of infant mortality data between linked file and vital statistics mortality file

The overall infant mortality rate from the 2008 period linked file of 6.61 is the same as from the 2008 vital statistics mortality file (4). The number of infant deaths in the linked file (28,075) differs slightly from the number in the mortality file (28,059) (4). Differences in numbers of infant deaths between the two data sources are primarily due to geographic coverage differences. For the vital statistics mortality file, all deaths occurring in the 50 states and DC are included regardless of the place of birth of the infant. In contrast, to be included in the U.S. linked file, both the birth and death must occur in the 50 states and DC (the territory linked file is a separate file). Weighting of the linked file also may contribute to small differences in numbers and rates by specific variables between these two data sets.

Table I. Percentage of infant death records that were linked to their corresponding birth records: United States and each state, Puerto Rico, Virgin Islands, and Guam, 2008 linked file

State	Percent linked by state of occurrence of death
United States[1]	98.7
Alabama	100.0
Alaska	98.4
Arizona	97.5
Arkansas	100.0
California	97.5
Colorado	100.0
Connecticut	100.0
Delaware	100.0
District of Columbia	98.2
Florida	99.8
Georgia	98.6
Hawaii	100.0
Idaho	100.0
Illinois	98.7
Indiana	99.7
Iowa	99.5
Kansas	100.0
Kentucky	99.4
Louisiana	96.0
Maine	100.0
Maryland	100.0
Massachusetts	100.0
Michigan	99.7
Minnesota	100.0
Mississippi	99.5
Missouri	99.3
Montana	100.0
Nebraska	99.4
Nevada	100.0
New Hampshire	100.0
New Jersey	98.9
New Mexico	98.1
New York (excluding New York city)	100.0
New York city	99.3
North Carolina	99.7
North Dakota	100.0
Ohio	98.6
Oklahoma	97.7
Oregon	99.6
Pennsylvania	99.8
Rhode Island	98.8
South Carolina	100.0
South Dakota	100.0
Tennessee	100.0
Texas	95.0
Utah	96.2
Vermont	100.0
Virginia	99.3
Washington	100.0
West Virginia	99.4
Wisconsin	99.8
Wyoming	100.0
Puerto Rico	98.7
Virgin Islands	75.0
Guam	93.3

[1]Excludes data for Puerto Rico, Virgin Islands, and Guam.

1989 and 2003 revisions of U.S. Standard Certificates of Live Birth

This report includes 2008 data on items that are collected on both the 1989 revision of the U.S. Standard Certificate of Live Birth (unrevised) and the 2003 revision of the U.S. Standard Certificate of Live Birth (revised) (3). The 2003 revision is described in detail elsewhere (48–50).

Maternal education, prenatal care, and smoking during pregnancy

Data for educational attainment, prenatal care, and tobacco use, although collected on both the revised and unrevised birth certificates, are not considered comparable between revisions. Because the 2008 linked file has birth records from both 2007 and 2008, the reporting areas of these three items from the 2003 revised certificate are those that revised by January 1, 2007. Twenty-two states had implemented the revised birth certificate by January 1, 2007: California, Colorado, Delaware, Florida, Idaho, Indiana, Iowa, Kansas, Kentucky, Nebraska, New Hampshire, New York (excluding New York city), North Dakota, Ohio, Pennsylvania, South Carolina, South Dakota, Tennessee, Texas, Vermont, Washington, and Wyoming. Data for Florida are excluded in the smoking results because the state's birth certificate question on smoking is not comparable to the 2003 revision (3).

However, maternal education, prenatal care, and smoking during pregnancy continue to have important relationships with infant mortality, with higher rates for smokers, women with late or no prenatal care, and those with less than a high school education (Table II). Analyses of these important variables will be expanded when all states adopt the 2003 revision.

Table II. Infant mortality rates for 2008, by trimester when pregnancy prenatal care began, smoking status during pregnancy, and education of mother: 22-state reporting area as of January 1, 2007

[Rates per 1,000 live births in specified group]

Characteristic	Rate
Prenatal care.	
Prenatal care beginning in the 1st trimester	5.31
Prenatal care beginning after the 1st trimester or no care. . .	7.37
Prenatal care beginning in the 2nd trimester	6.09
Prenatal care beginning in the 3rd trimester.	5.60
No prenatal care.	27.25
Smoking status:	
Smoker.	9.68
Nonsmoker	5.68
Educational attainment:	
Less than high school diploma.	7.74
High school diploma	7.22
Some college or technical school	5.71
Bachelor's degree or higher	3.74

NOTES: Includes data from California, Colorado, Delaware, Florida, Idaho, Indiana, Iowa, Kansas, Kentucky, Nebraska, New Hampshire, New York (excluding New York city), North Dakota, Ohio, Pennsylvania, South Carolina, South Dakota, Tennessee, Texas, Vermont, Washington, and Wyoming. These states are those that revised their birth certificates as of January 1, 2007. Information on smoking status excludes data for Florida. See "Methods" and "Technical Notes."

Marital status

National estimates of births to unmarried women are based on two methods of determining marital status. In 2008, marital status was based on a direct question in 48 states and DC. In the two states that used inferential procedures to compile birth statistics by marital status (Michigan and New York), a birth is inferred as nonmarital if either of the following factors, listed in priority-of-use order, is present: a paternity acknowledgment was received or the father's name is missing (3).

Multiple race

For the birth certificates in the 2008 data year, multiple race was reported by 30 states (both revised and unrevised): California, Colorado, Delaware, Florida, Georgia, Hawaii, Idaho, Indiana, Iowa, Kansas, Kentucky, Michigan, Minnesota, Montana, Nebraska, New Hampshire, New Mexico, New York (excluding New York city), North Dakota, Ohio, Oregon, Pennsylvania, South Carolina, South Dakota, Tennessee, Texas, Utah, Vermont, Washington, and Wyoming (3). Twenty-seven states reported multiple race in 2007 (51). Data from the vital records of the remaining states, DC, and New York city followed 1977 Office of Management and Budget standards in which a single race is reported (52,53). In addition, these areas also report the minimum set of four races as stipulated in the 1977 standards, compared with the minimum of five races mandated by the 1997 standards (3).

To provide uniformity and comparability of the data during the transition period, before multiple-race data are available for all reporting areas, the responses of those who reported more than one race are bridged to a single race. Multiple race is imputed to a single race (American Indian or Alaska Native, Asian or Pacific Islander, black, or white) according to the combination of races, Hispanic origin, sex, and age indicated on the birth certificate using methods described elsewhere (3,9,54).

Period of gestation

The primary measure used to determine the gestational age of the newborn is the interval between the first day of the mother's last normal menstrual period (LMP) and the date of birth. It is subject to error for several reasons, including imperfect maternal recall or misidentification of the LMP because of postconception bleeding, delayed ovulation, or intervening early miscarriage. When the LMP date was not reported or was inconsistent with birthweight, the "obstetric estimate of gestation" was used (6 percent of births) (2,3).

Birthweight

For the linked file, not-stated birthweight was imputed for 3,391 records, or 0.08 percent of the birth records in 2008 when birthweight was not stated but the period of gestation was known. In this case, birthweight was assigned the value from the previous record with the same period of gestation, maternal race, sex, and plurality. If birthweight and period of gestation were both unknown, the not-stated value for birthweight was retained. This imputation was done to improve the accuracy of birthweight-specific infant mortality rates, because the percentage of records with not-stated birthweight was higher for infant deaths (3.26 percent before imputation) than for live births (0.10 percent before imputation). The imputation reduced the percentage of not-stated records to 0.48 percent for infant deaths, and 0.02 percent for births. The not-stated birthweight cases in the natality/birth file, as distinct from the linked file, are not imputed (3).

Cause-of-death classification

The mortality statistics presented in this report were compiled in accordance with World Health Organization (WHO) regulations, which specify that member nations classify and code causes of death in accordance with the current revision of the *International Statistical Classification of Diseases and Related Health Problems* (ICD). The ICD provides the basic guidance used in virtually all countries to code and classify causes of death. The ICD not only details disease classification but also provides definitions, tabulation lists, the format of the death certificate, and the rules for coding cause of death. Cause-of-death data presented in this report were coded by procedures outlined in annual issues of the *NCHS Instruction Manual* (55,56).

In this report, tabulations of cause-of-death statistics are based solely on the underlying cause of death. The underlying cause is defined by WHO as "the disease or injury which initiated the train of morbid events leading directly to death, or the circumstances of the accident or violence which produced the fatal injury" (5). Cause of death is selected from the conditions entered by the physician in the cause-of-death section of the death certificate. When more than one cause or condition is entered by the physician, the underlying cause is determined by the sequence of conditions on the certificate, ICD provisions, and associated selection and modification rules. Generally, more medical information is reported on death certificates than is directly reflected in the underlying cause of death. This is captured in NCHS multiple cause-of-death statistics (57,58).

About every 10–20 years, the ICD is revised to take into account advances in medical knowledge. Effective with deaths occurring in 1999, the United States began using the ICD's Tenth Revision (ICD–10) (5); during the 1979–1998 period, causes were coded and classified according to the Ninth Revision (ICD–9) (59).

Changes in cause-of-death classification due to these revisions may result in discontinuities in cause-of-death trends. Measures of this discontinuity are essential to the interpretation of mortality trends and are discussed in detail in other NCHS publications (4,60,61).

Tabulation lists and cause-of-death ranking

The cause-of-death rankings for ICD–10 are based on the List of 130 Selected Causes of Infant Death. The tabulation lists and rules for ranking leading causes of death are published in the NCHS *Instruction Manual, Part 9, ICD–10 Cause-of-Death Lists for Tabulating Mortality Statistics, Effective 1999* (62). Briefly, category titles that begin with the words "Other" and "All other" are not ranked to determine the leading causes of death. When one of the titles that represents a subtotal is ranked [for example, Influenza and pneumonia (J10–J18)], its component parts are not ranked [in this case, Influenza (J10–J11) and Pneumonia (J12–18)].

Preterm-related causes of death

Preterm-related causes of death are those causes that have a direct etiological connection to preterm birth. For an underlying cause of death to be considered preterm-related, 75 percent or more of infants whose deaths were attributed to that cause had to be born preterm, and the cause of death had to be a direct consequence of preterm birth based on a clinical evaluation and review of the literature (45). The cause-of-death categories included in this grouping are shown in the Table 6 footnote. Causes that are incidental to preterm birth (for example, Motor vehicle accident to a preterm infant) are not included. This grouping of preterm-related causes probably underestimates the total impact of preterm-related infant death, as some ICD categories (notably those beginning with the words "Other" and "All other") had a high percentage of preterm infant deaths but lacked sufficient specificity to be able to establish the etiologic connection to prematurity with any degree of certainty. Further details on the development of this cause-of-death grouping are available in related publications (45,46).

Computation of rates

Infant mortality rates are the most commonly used index for measuring the risk of dying during the first year of life. For the linked birth/infant death data set, they are calculated by dividing the number of infant deaths in a calendar year by the number of live births registered for the same period and are presented as rates per 1,000 or per 100,000 live births. Both the mortality file and the linked birth/infant death file use this computation method, but due to unique numbers of infant deaths (as explained in the section above on the comparison of these two files), the rates will often differ for specific variables, particularly for race and ethnicity. Infant mortality rates in the linked file use the number of live births in the denominator to approximate the population at risk of dying before the first birthday. In contrast to the infant mortality rates based on live births, infant death rates, used only in age-specific death rates with the mortality file, use the estimated population of persons under age 1 year as the denominator.

For all variables, not-stated responses were shown in tables of frequencies, but were dropped before rates were computed. Rates per 1,000 live births display two digits after the decimal place to provide a more precise and sensitive measurement. For rates per 100,000 live births (by cause of death), the infant mortality rate is shown for one decimal place. Adding another decimal for rates per 100,000 does not increase precision as it does for rates per 1,000.

As stated previously, infant death records for the 50 states and DC in the U.S. linked file are weighted so that the infant mortality rates are not underestimated for those areas that did not successfully link all records.

Random variation in infant mortality rates

The number of infant deaths and live births reported for an area represent complete counts of such events. As such, they are not subject to sampling error, although they are subject to nonsampling error in the registration process. However, when the figures are used for analytic purposes, such as the comparison of rates over time, for different areas, or among different subgroups, the number of events that actually occurred may be considered as one of a large series of possible results that could have arisen under the same circumstances (63). As a result, numbers of births, deaths, and infant mortality rates are subject to random variation. The probable range of values may be estimated from the actual figures according to certain statistical assumptions.

In general, distributions of vital events may be assumed to follow the normal distribution. When the number of events is large, the relative standard error (RSE) is usually small. When the number of events is small (perhaps less than 100) and the probability of such an event is small, considerable caution must be observed in interpreting the data. Such infrequent events may be assumed to follow a Poisson probability distribution (3,4). Estimates of RSEs and 95 percent confidence intervals are shown below.

The formula for the RSE of infant deaths and live births is:

$$RSE(D) = 100 \cdot \sqrt{\frac{1}{D}},$$

where D is the number of deaths, and

$$RSE(B) = 100 \cdot \sqrt{\frac{1}{B}},$$

where B is the number of births.

For example, suppose that for group A, the number of infant deaths was 497, while the number of live births was 81,555, yielding an infant mortality rate of 6.09 infant deaths per 1,000 live births.

$$\text{The RSE of the deaths} = 100 \cdot \sqrt{\frac{1}{497}} = 4.49,$$

$$\text{while the RSE of the births} = 100 \cdot \sqrt{\frac{1}{81,555}} = 0.35.$$

The formula for the RSE of the infant mortality rate (IMR) is:

$$RSE(IMR) = 100 \cdot \sqrt{\frac{1}{D} + \frac{1}{B}}.$$

The RSE of the IMR for the example above

$$= 100 \cdot \sqrt{\frac{1}{497} + \frac{1}{81,555}} = 4.50.$$

Normal distribution—When the number of events is greater than 100, the normal distribution is used to estimate the 95 percent confidence intervals as follows:

$$\text{Lower: } R_1 - 1.96 \cdot R_1 \cdot \frac{RSE(R_1)}{100}.$$

$$\text{Upper: } R_1 + 1.96 \cdot R_1 \cdot \frac{RSE(R_1)}{100}.$$

Thus, for Group A:

$$\text{Lower: } 6.09 - \left(1.96 \cdot 6.09 \cdot \frac{4.50}{100}\right) = 5.55.$$

$$\text{Upper: } 6.09 + \left(1.96 \cdot 6.09 \cdot \frac{4.50}{100}\right) = 6.63.$$

The chances are 95 out of 100 that the true IMR for group A lies somewhere in the 5.55–6.63 interval.

Poisson distribution—When the number of events in the numerator is less than 100, the confidence interval for the rate can be estimated based on the Poisson distribution using the values in Table III.

$$\text{Lower: IMR} \cdot L(0.95, D_{adj})$$

$$\text{Upper: IMR} \cdot U(0.95, D_{adj}),$$

where D_{adj} is the adjusted number of infant deaths (rounded to the nearest integer) used to take into account the RSE of the number of infant deaths and live births, and is computed as:

$$D_{adj} = \frac{D \cdot B}{D + B}.$$

$L(0.95, D_{adj})$ and $U(0.95, D_{adj})$ refer to the values in Table III corresponding to the value of D_{adj}.

For example, suppose that for group B the number of infant deaths was 53, the number of live births was 9,241, and the infant mortality rate was 5.74.

$$D_{adj} = \frac{53 \cdot 9,241}{53 + 9,241} = 53.$$

Therefore, the 95 percent confidence interval (using the formula in Table III for 1–99 infant deaths) is:

$$\text{Lower: } 5.74 \cdot 0.74907 = 4.30.$$

$$\text{Upper: } 5.74 \cdot 1.30802 = 7.51.$$

Comparison of two infant mortality rates—If either of the two rates to be compared is based on fewer than 100 deaths, compute the confidence intervals for both rates and check to see if they overlap. If so, the difference is not statistically significant at the 95 percent level. If they do not overlap, the difference is statistically significant. If both of the two rates (R_1 and R_2) to be compared are based on 100 or more deaths, the following z test may be used to define a significance test statistic:

$$z = \frac{R_1 - R_2}{\sqrt{R_1^2 \left(\frac{RSE(R_1)}{100}\right)^2 + R_2^2 \left(\frac{RSE(R_2)}{100}\right)^2}}$$

If $|z|$ is greater than or equal to 1.96, then the difference is statistically significant at the 0.05 level, and if $|z|$ is less than 1.96, the difference is not significant.

Availability of linked file data

Linked file data are available for download at http://www.cdc.gov/nchs/data_access/VitalStatsOnline.htm. Beginning with 2005, the public-use file no longer includes geographic detail; such files are available upon special request (see http://www.cdc.gov/nchs/nvss/dvs_data_release.htm). Prebuilt tables are available from http://www.cdc.gov/nchs/VitalStats.htm. Data are also available in issues of Vital and Health Statistics, Series 20, National Vital Statistics Reports, and Data Briefs from http://www.cdc.gov/nchs/.

Table III. Values of *L* and *U* for calculating 95 percent confidence limits for numbers of events and rates when the number of events is less than 100

N	L	U	N	L	U
1	0.02532	5.57164	51	0.74457	1.31482
2	0.12110	3.61234	52	0.74685	1.31137
3	0.20622	2.92242	53	0.74907	1.30802
4	0.27247	2.56040	54	0.75123	1.30478
5	0.32470	2.33367	55	0.75334	1.30164
6	0.36698	2.17658	56	0.75539	1.29858
7	0.40205	2.06038	57	0.75739	1.29562
8	0.43173	1.97040	58	0.75934	1.29273
9	0.45726	1.89831	59	0.76125	1.28993
10	0.47954	1.83904	60	0.76311	1.28720
11	0.49920	1.78928	61	0.76492	1.28454
12	0.51671	1.74680	62	0.76669	1.28195
13	0.53246	1.71003	63	0.76843	1.27943
14	0.54671	1.67783	64	0.77012	1.27698
15	0.55969	1.64935	65	0.77178	1.27458
16	0.57159	1.62394	66	0.77340	1.27225
17	0.58254	1.60110	67	0.77499	1.26996
18	0.59266	1.58043	68	0.77654	1.26774
19	0.60207	1.56162	69	0.77806	1.26556
20	0.61083	1.54442	70	0.77955	1.26344
21	0.61902	1.52861	71	0.78101	1.26136
22	0.62669	1.51401	72	0.78244	1.25933
23	0.63391	1.50049	73	0.78384	1.25735
24	0.64072	1.48792	74	0.78522	1.25541
25	0.64715	1.47620	75	0.78656	1.25351
26	0.65323	1.46523	76	0.78789	1.25165
27	0.65901	1.45495	77	0.78918	1.24983
28	0.66449	1.44528	78	0.79046	1.24805
29	0.66972	1.43617	79	0.79171	1.24630
30	0.67470	1.42756	80	0.79294	1.24459
31	0.67945	1.41942	81	0.79414	1.24291
32	0.68400	1.41170	82	0.79533	1.24126
33	0.68835	1.40437	83	0.79649	1.23965
34	0.69253	1.39740	84	0.79764	1.23807
35	0.69654	1.39076	85	0.79876	1.23652
36	0.70039	1.38442	86	0.79987	1.23499
37	0.70409	1.37837	87	0.80096	1.23350
38	0.70766	1.37258	88	0.80203	1.23203
39	0.71110	1.36703	89	0.80308	1.23059
40	0.71441	1.36172	90	0.80412	1.22917
41	0.71762	1.35661	91	0.80514	1.22778
42	0.72071	1.35171	92	0.80614	1.22641
43	0.72370	1.34699	93	0.80713	1.22507
44	0.72660	1.34245	94	0.80810	1.22375
45	0.72941	1.33808	95	0.80906	1.22245
46	0.73213	1.33386	96	0.81000	1.22117
47	0.73476	1.32979	97	0.81093	1.21992
48	0.73732	1.32585	98	0.81185	1.21868
49	0.73981	1.32205	99	0.81275	1.21746
50	0.74222	1.31838			

**U.S. DEPARTMENT OF
HEALTH & HUMAN SERVICES**

Centers for Disease Control and Prevention
National Center for Health Statistics
3311 Toledo Road
Hyattsville, MD 20782

OFFICIAL BUSINESS
PENALTY FOR PRIVATE USE, $300

National Vital Statistics Reports, Vol. 60, No. 5, May 10, 2012

Contents

Abstract 2
Introduction 2
Methods. 2
   Data by maternal and infant characteristics. 3
Results and Discussion. 3
   Trends in infant mortality 3
   Infant mortality by race and Hispanic origin of mother 3
   Age at death. 4
   Infant mortality by state, and by race and ethnicity 5
   Sex of infant. 6
   Multiple births 6
   Period of gestation 7
   Birthweight 8
   Maternal age. 8
   Live-birth order 8
   Marital status 8
   Nativity 8
   Leading causes of infant death. 9
   Preterm-related causes of death 10
References 11
List of Detailed Tables. 13
Technical Notes. 23

Acknowledgments

This report was prepared under the general direction of Charles J. Rothwell, Director of the Division of Vital Statistics, and Stephanie J. Ventura, Chief of the Reproductive Statistics Branch. Nicholas Pace, Chief of Systems, Programming, and Statistical Resources Branch (SPSRB), Steve Steimel, Candace Cosgrove, and John Birken (SPSRB) provided computer programming support and statistical tables. Yashu Patel of RSB provided assistance with content review. The Registration Methods staff and the Data Acquisition and Evaluation Branch provided consultation to state vital statistics offices regarding collection of the birth and death certificate data on which this report is based. The report was edited and produced by CDC/OSELS/NCHS/OD/Office of Information Services, Information Design and Publishing Staff: Betsy M. Finley edited the report; typesetting was done by Annette F. Holman; and graphics were produced by Ryan M. Dumas (contractor).

Suggested citation

Mathews TJ, MacDorman MF. Infant mortality statistics from the 2008 period linked birth/infant death data set. National vital statistics reports; vol 60 no 5. Hyattsville, MD: National Center for Health Statistics. 2012.

National Center for Health Statistics

Edward J. Sondik, Ph.D., *Director*
Jennifer H. Madans, Ph.D., *Associate Director
for Science*

Division of Vital Statistics
Charles J. Rothwell, M.S., *Director*

For e-mail updates on NCHS publication releases, subscribe online at: http://www.cdc.gov/nchs/govdelivery.htm.
For questions or general information about NCHS: Tel: 1–800–232–4636 • E-mail: cdcinfo@cdc.gov • Internet: http://www.cdc.gov/nchs
DHHS Publication No. (PHS) 2012–1120 • CS232928